etzoff, Carole
...atural cook's
...st book

THE NATURAL COOK'S
FIRST BOOK

THE NATURAL COOK'S
A Natural Foods

CAROLE GETZOFF

Illustrated by JILL PINKWATER

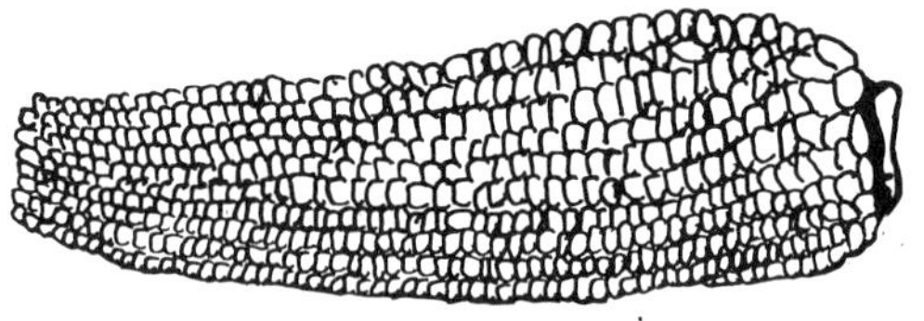

FIRST BOOK
Cookbook for Beginners

DODD, MEAD & COMPANY · New York

For Stephen—
just because . . .

CONTENTS

BREAKFAST

A WORD TO ANY ADULT WHO MIGHT BE SNEAKING A GLANCE AT THIS BOOK

This book was born out of a righteous feeling for children. While there are hundreds of books for adults which instruct how to cook with pure, whole foods, kids still have to put up with cookbooks that feed them recipes for green iced cupcakes and other giggly foods with no substance. Children deserve more serious consideration.

Much of this book grew out of a cooking class I taught in which four eight- and nine-year-olds participated. I learned a lot in that class. Perhaps the most important thing I learned was to trust the clear and intuitive connection that children have with food. Their tastes are definite. They know what they like and what they don't like. The recipes that turned them on form the bulk of this book.

Aside from the simple preparation and pleasing tastes, the recipes were designed with two other considerations in mind—that they be healthy and fun to cook, too.

As for your part in the use of this book, I suggest that you supervise rather than assist your child in the kitchen. There are certain tasks children may need help with such as lighting the oven or cutting a particularly hard substance, but on the whole this book is designed for children to cook independently of adults.

I hope this book sparks creativity in the kitchen. It seems to me that children and cooking naturally go so well together that the result can't help but be exciting experiences as well as delicious food.

INTRODUCTION

This is a book that was written especially for children. Not for aunts and uncles or cats and dogs or mothers and fathers but for children. Some of their names are Jonathan and Paul and Binky and Claudia.

This book is for children who like to play, ride bikes, skate, run, play basketball, read books, fly kites, swim, skip, laugh, and eat good food. I hope that means you.

When I was young I didn't like to eat. I especially didn't like to eat vegetables or rice or anything that was good for me. But that was because everything that was good for me didn't taste very good. When I grew up I found out how to make food that was good for me taste good, too. And now I love vegetables. I could practically eat a vegetable sundae, I love vegetables so much. And I love rice and cereals, too. I bet you don't believe it. Well, try some of the recipes in this book and see if the same thing doesn't happen to you.

I never liked to eat, but I always loved to cook. Cooking to me is like painting with pots and pans and spoons and bowls in colors like broccoli green and carrot orange and red cabbage purple. But the great thing about cooking is that when you've finished your masterpiece you don't have to hang it on the wall and just look at it. You can look at it and then eat it.

This is a book about a certain kind of food called natural food. Now you may be wondering what on earth is natural food. And that's just it. Natural food is food that grows in the earth with the help of the sun and the rain and the people who plant the seed and take care of the plant. For example, a carrot is a natural food but a TV dinner isn't. A TV dinner does not grow in the earth. It is made in a factory by machines and chemicals.

The recipes in this book use only natural ingredients because: (1) Natural foods are good for you and taste good, too. (2) They're fun to cook. (3) I like them and I'm the one who got to write the book.

I've said enough. Now it's time to see for yourself. Remember to read the directions carefully and to always be careful when you cook. I know that some of the things I've said you're probably going to forget. But please don't forget the one most important thing. That's to have a good time.

THE NATURAL COOK'S FIRST BOOK

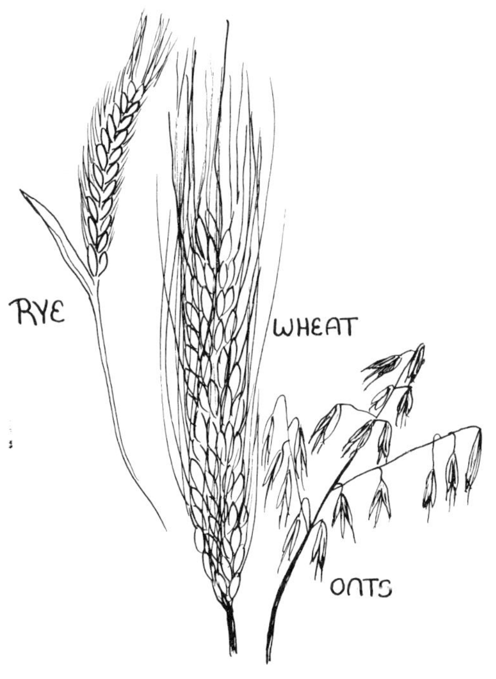

EQUIVALENTS OR WHAT-EQUALS-WHAT TABLE

3	teaspoons	=	1	tablespoon
4	tablespoons	=	¼	cup
2	cups	=	1	pint
16	ounces (liquid)	=	1	pint
16	ounces (dry)	=	1	pound
2	pints	=	1	quart
4	quarts	=	1	gallon
1	dozen	=	12	

NEW FOODS THAT ARE REALLY OLD

Many of the foods in this book may be new to you, but they are really very old. *Grains* have been on this earth for thousands of years. *Tamari* soy sauce is another food that people have been using in the Orient for a long time. You probably already know what soy sauce is. It is the black liquid that you sometimes put on your food in Chinese restaurants. Tamari is the best, but if it's not available, use the best soy sauce you can find or the one with the least artificial ingredients. Tamari soy sauce is special because it is made with fermented or "over-ripe" soybeans, wheat, sea salt, and water. Nothing else. It is good to use when you want to add a special kind of salty flavor to your food. It is also good for you because it has protein in it. Remember to use just a little in your food. A few drops go a long way. A small bottle like the one used in Chinese restaurants to pour soy sauce is a good bottle to keep your tamari in. This helps you to use a little at a time.

In all the recipes that use salt, I suggest you try *sea salt*. Sea salt is a pure salt that comes from the sea and has not been refined or changed. It is good for you because it has important minerals like magnesium in it. Again, remember not to use too much. A few drops of sea salt go a long way, too.

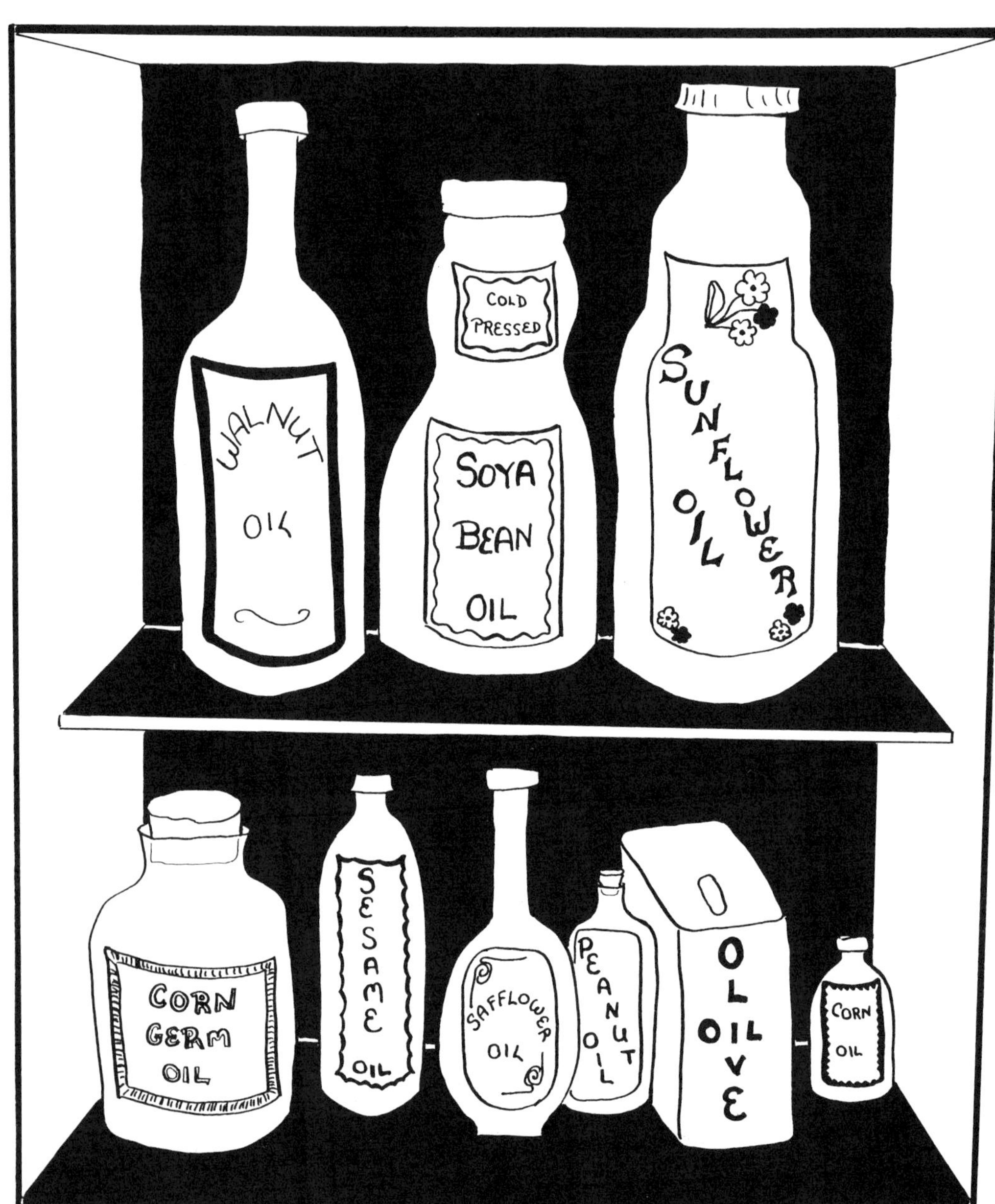

WALNUT OIL
COLD PRESSED
SOYA BEAN OIL
SUNFLOWER OIL
CORN GERM OIL
SESAME OIL
SAFFLOWER OIL
PEANUT OIL
OLIVE OIL
CORN OIL

THE SLIPPERY SIDE OF THINGS: ALL ABOUT OIL

In most of the recipes in this book, I suggest you use pure vegetable oil rather than butter. There are many reasons for this. One is that I like to use foods that come from vegetables rather than ones that come from animals. Pure oils that are squeezed from vegetables and seeds like corn oil, corn germ oil, sesame oil, and safflower oil are good for you. This is because they are "unsaturated" and have "essential fatty acids" in them that help you to be healthy. Fats that come from animals are "saturated." Saturated fats are *not* good for you because they raise the cholesterol level of the blood. Many doctors think this helps cause heart disease.

Try to use oils that are *cold pressed.* Cold pressing is a way of making oil without heating it first. This also saves the vitamins and minerals in it.

Also try to use *unrefined* oils. When oil is refined it becomes tired because the strong vitamins are taken out of it.

Use oil sparingly when you cook. Like tamari, a little oil goes a long way.

Try to use:　1. *pure vegetable* and *seed oils* that are
　　　　　　 2. *cold pressed* and
　　　　　　 3. *unrefined.*

ADUKI BEANS
SESAME SEEDS
RAISINS
SEA SALT
TAMARI
LIMA BEANS
CHINESE MUSHROOMS
PINTO BEANS
TAHINI
BULGHUR
MILLET
WHOLE WHEAT NOODLES
OATS
BROWN RICE

GRAINS

Grains—oats, rye, corn, millet, rice, barley, and wheat—come in all different shapes and sizes. There are grains that are made by cutting up whole grains. Bulghur wheat is a cut grain. There are grains that are made by cracking whole grains. Cracked wheat is an example of this. There are also grains that are made by grinding whole grains. These grains are called flours.

Whole grains are the best grains because they have so many vitamins and minerals stored inside them. As soon as you cut or crack or grind a grain, the vitamins and minerals begin to leak out just like the air in a flat tire. That is why it is important to make sure these grains are fresh when you use them. The fresher they are, the healthier they are. Whole grains can last forever without losing their vitamins and minerals.

Most grains are changed a great deal before we get to use them. A good example of this is white rice. A grain of rice grows with three layers called the bran, the rice polish, and the germ. In order to make rice white, the bran and rice polish are taken away and only the germ is left. This means that white rice is missing important vitamins and minerals. That is why brown rice is healthier for you. Brown rice is the whole grain of rice. It has all three layers. Brown rice also has a crunchy nutty flavor which I'm sure you'll like. Try to use brown rice whenever you make rice.

There are also other things that are done to grains to change them. For instance, flour is bleached to make it look whiter. Bleached flour is not very good for you because the bleach hurts the vitamin E in the flour.

The way in which the flour is ground is also very important. Most flour is ground in a way that uses a very high heat. Heat hurts vitamins. That is why it is good to buy flour that has been *stoneground*. This is a way of making flour that grinds the grain between two stones. The American Indians used to grind their flour this way. The good thing about stone-grinding is that it uses less heat and saves more vitamins.

You can grind a flour so that it is smooth and light. You can also grind a flour so that it has small pieces of grain in it and is heavier. *Finely* ground flour, like whole wheat pastry flour, is used to make desserts. *Coarsely* ground flour, like regular whole wheat flour, is used to make bread. You can choose the kind of grind you need.

When you buy flours try to keep three things in mind. The best flours to use are:

1. *whole grain flours*
2. *unbleached flours*
3. *stoneground flours*

VEGETABLES

Vegetables are really a treat. They're pretty, come in bright colors, are dancing with vitamins, and taste good, too. They grow in gardens right in the earth. The really amazing thing about them is that there are so many kinds. Here are some of the ones I like best: asparagus, carrots, onions, Chinese cabbage, red or purple cabbage, green cabbage, butternut squash, Hubbard squash, acorn squash, zucchini squash, scallions, radishes, parsnips, kale, broccoli, cauliflower, green peppers, string beans, green peas, mushrooms, watercress, parsley, spinach, turnips, corn on the cob, and special ones like burdock, lotus root, and daikon (Japanese radish).

When you cook them, it is a good idea to cook a combination of three, like onions, broccoli, and carrots.

You can buy most of these vegetables in any grocery store or supermarket. Get them as fresh as you can. Vegetables that come from your local area are good to use. Fresh vegetables taste much better and are much better for you than the ones that come in cans or frozen packages. Vegetables that come in cans have usually been cooked for a long time, which means they're missing vitamins. Besides, the tin vegetables come in is not very good for you. Frozen vegetables might have more vitamins left than canned vege-

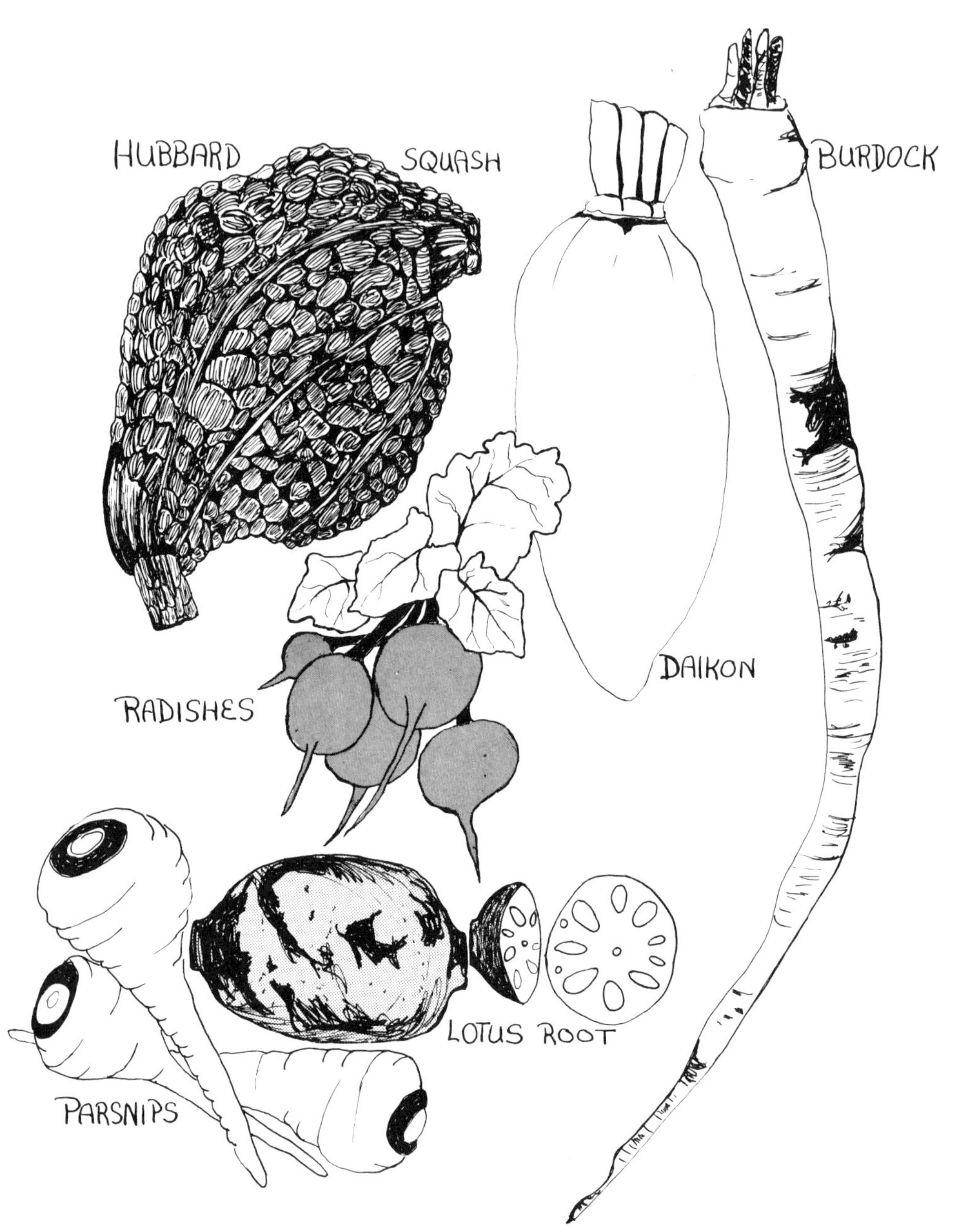
HUBBARD
SQUASH
BURDOCK
DAIKON
RADISHES
LOTUS ROOT
PARSNIPS

tables, but the very best you can buy are fresh vegetables. The same goes for fruits.

It's also good to remember to buy fruits and vegetables in the season they are grown. For instance, buy strawberries in the summer, not in the winter.

Have you ever heard of *organic* vegetables? Organic vegetables are grown without using chemicals or sprays that might be bad for you. Farmers use these chemicals because they keep insects from eating the plants while they are growing. Certain chemicals also make vegetables grow bigger or faster. The bad part about these chemicals is that they don't wash off.

Not all farmers use strong chemicals to grow their vegetables. These farmers grow organic vegetables. I think organic vegetables taste better and are better for you. But there is one thing that is bad about organic vegetables. Only a few farmers grow them, so they are more expensive to buy. If you buy fresh vegetables that are not organic, remember to scrub them well with a vegetable brush. Try not to peel them because the vegetable skin has vitamins in it.

When you buy vegetables remember to buy *fresh vegetables* instead of canned or frozen ones.

SMALL THINGS
TO REMEMBER

1. Buy real food instead of fake or imitation food.
2. Be sure to read each recipe carefully before starting to cook.
3. Use dry potholders for hot pots.
4. Pay attention to what you're cooking. If you leave the kitchen in the middle of making a dish, check back in on what's cooking every few minutes.
5. Ask an adult for help when you need it.
6. Don't rush. Calm cooks make calm food.
7. Save the water left over from cooking to use when you cook other foods.
8. Eat slowly. Eating is not a race.
9. Raw nuts are better for you than roasted nuts.
10. There is a difference between Chinese and Japanese chopsticks. Chinese chopsticks have thick round edges and are longer than Japanese chopsticks. Japanese chopsticks have one pointy end.
11. Clean as you cook. The mess will be less.
12. Save leftovers by putting them into the refrigerator in a covered bowl or container.
13. Ask an adult for permission or help when turning on the oven.

WHERE TO BUY FOOD

Many of the foods used in the recipes in this book can be bought in a supermarket or grocery store.

Some of the special foods will probably have to be bought in a health food store. These foods are sea salt, tamari, arrowroot, agar agar, and Chinese mushrooms. Some of the others, such as herb teas, might be found in a good super-market or grocery store. These foods are pure vegetable and seed oils, unhulled sesame seeds, tahini, brown rice, bulghur, millet, oats, whole wheat noodles, whole grain flours, and beans.

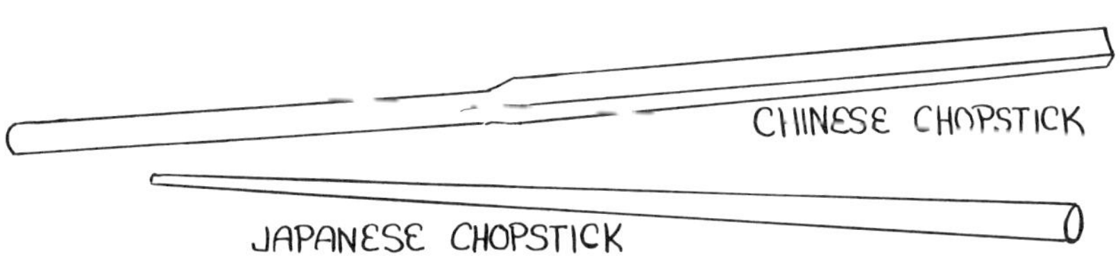

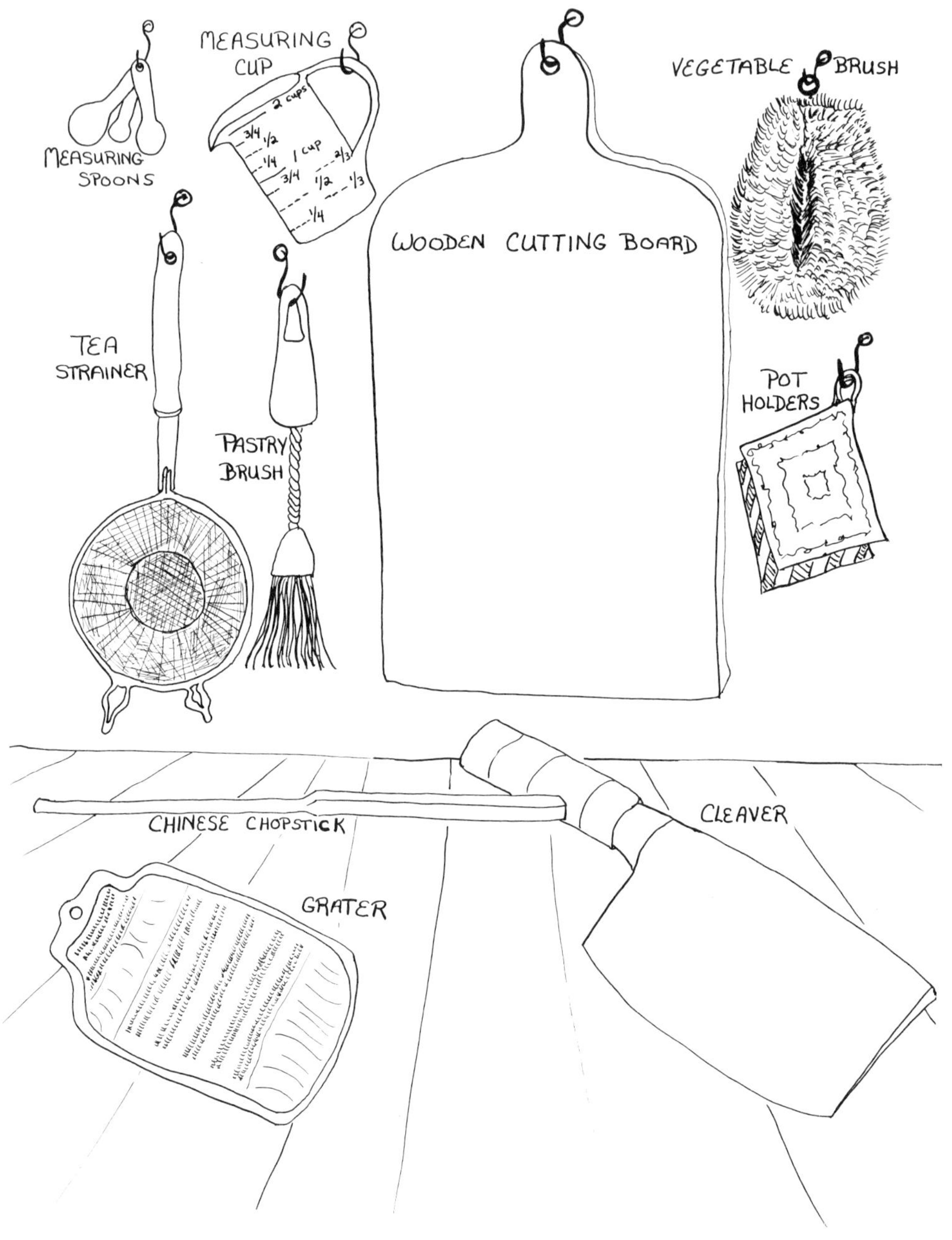

MEASURING SPOONS
MEASURING CUP
2 cups
3/4 1/2
1/4 1 cup 2/3
3/4 1/2 1/3
1/4
VEGETABLE BRUSH
WOODEN CUTTING BOARD
POT HOLDERS
TEA STRAINER
PASTRY BRUSH
CHINESE CHOPSTICK
GRATER
CLEAVER

GADGETS THAT HELP YOU COOK

These are a few items very useful to have in your kitchen. Most of them (except the pots) are not expensive and are simple to use.

1. a set of measuring spoons
2. a measuring cup (a 2-cup measure is a good size)
3. a set of 3 mixing bowls (small, medium, and large)
4. a wooden spoon
5. a Chinese wooden chopstick for stirring
6. a cleaver or sharp broad knife
7. a wooden cutting board
8. a set of heavy pots and pans made out of either stainless steel, enameled ironware, or earthenware. Try not to use aluminum. Useful sizes are 7- and 8½-inch saucepans and a 10-inch skillet (all with covers).
9. a grater
10. a pastry brush
11. a scrub brush for vegetables
12. 1 or 2 cookie sheets (11 inches by 16 inches)
13. an egg beater or electric mixer or blender
14. a tea strainer
15. 2 dry potholders

BREAKFAST

When I was a child, breakfast was the meal I liked least of all. That was because I thought breakfast had to be dull. Now, I wouldn't have minded eating exciting things like the "baobabs" the Little Prince ate or the funny berries Winnie the Pooh found in the forest. But dry cereals that come in boxes and tasteless bread practically make me go to sleep.

Not liking breakfast was a real dilemma because so many people said it was a very important meal. After all, it is the first meal you eat each day before starting out, so it has a lot to do with making that day a good one. Eating a good breakfast is like putting gasoline in an empty tank. Except that people don't get their energy from gasoline. They get it from vitamins and minerals. Nutrients are what make people go. The only way to keep your body full of nutrients is by eating good food at every meal. Especially in the morning.

In this section I hope you'll find some ways to help start the day with a smile and a burst of energy.

OATMEAL

Oatmeal is a cereal prepared from a grain called oats. It's a great food to start the day with, especially in cold weather. Oatmeal is also so full of vitamins it will give you a bowlful of energy.

Count on 30 minutes from start to finish

INGREDIENTS

    2 cups rolled oats
    4 cups water
    ½ teaspoon salt

YOU'LL ALSO NEED

    1 pot with cover (medium)
    1 mixing spoon
    1 measuring cup
    1 set measuring spoons

WHAT TO DO

1. Boil the water.
2. Lower the flame to medium.
3. Carefully add the oats. Stir.
4. Add salt.
5. Simmer with the cover on for about 20 minutes. Stir occasionally.
6. You may add honey, milk, butter, raisins, fresh fruit, apple butter or sesame salt to the oatmeal. It even tastes good plain.
7. You've made enough for 4 servings.

OUR OWN GRANOLA

This is a dry cereal that tastes like candy.

*Count on 2½ hours from start
to finish*

INGREDIENTS

  1 cup rolled oats
⅓ cup sesame seeds
⅓ cup cashews (raw if possible)
⅓ cup sunflower seeds
¼ cup peanuts
  2 tablespoons honey
  2 tablespoons corn oil
  2 tablespoons water
  2 tablespoons raisins
  1 teaspoon oil for cookie sheet

YOU'LL ALSO NEED

  1 bowl (large)
  1 bowl (small)
  1 cutting board
  1 knife
  1 large cookie sheet (11 inches by 16 inches or
     larger)
  1 pastry brush or piece of paper towel
  1 potholder

WHAT TO DO

1. Preheat oven to 300° F.
2. Carefully cut the peanuts and cashews into small pieces on the cutting board.
3. Mix all the dry ingredients except the raisins together in the large bowl.
4. In the small bowl mix the honey, oil, and water.
5. Pour the honey, oil, and water mixture over the dry ingredients. Mix it well.
6. Oil a cookie sheet (see directions p. 87).
7. Spread the mixture out on the cookie sheet.
8. Put the cookie sheet into the oven.
9. Let it bake for about 2 hours until the cereal is golden brown. Stir it occasionally to make sure it doesn't burn.
10. Using a potholder, take the cookie sheet out of the oven and let it cool for about 10 minutes.
11. Take the cereal off the cookie sheet and put it into a bowl. Mix in the raisins.
12. You may store the cereal in a jar. It stays fresh for many weeks. You probably won't get to keep it very long because people will eat it so fast.
13. You've made enough for a week of breakfasts and snacks. Eat it plain or with milk.

APPLE SAUCE JAM

You might also try this recipe and use cherries or strawberries instead of apples. If you want the jam to be less sweet, use ½ cup honey and mix it with ¼ cup water or apple juice.

Count on 25 minutes from start to finish

INGREDIENTS

    2 apples
  ¾ cup honey
  ¼ teaspoon salt

YOU'LL ALSO NEED

  1 potholder
  1 spoon
  1 apple corer
  1 peeler (optional)
  1 pot with cover (small)
  1 knife
  1 measuring cup
  1 set measuring spoons

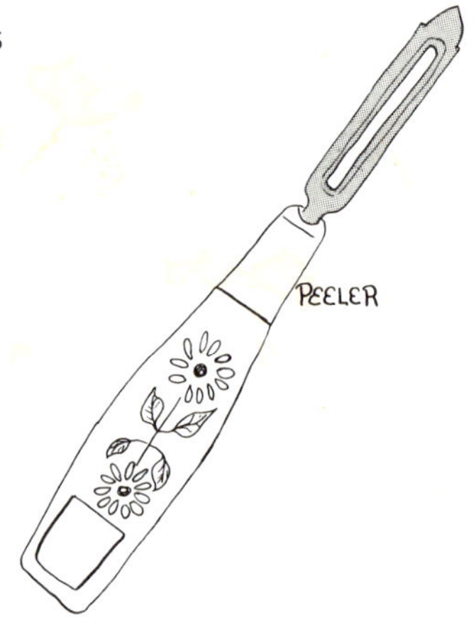

WHAT TO DO

1. Wash the apples. Peel them if you wish but it is not necessary. Core them. (See directions for How to Core an Apple, p. 86). Dice them into small pieces.
2. Put the honey into a pan. Place it over a medium flame. Add diced apples and salt.
3. Cook the apple mixture covered for 15 minutes. Every few minutes lift the cover with a potholder and stir.
4. Makes enough for 4 servings. Serve over pancakes or spread it on whole grain bread.

APPLE FRITTERS

You can try this recipe with blueberries, strawberries, or peaches instead of apples.

These fritters will take longer to cook than pancakes that have baking soda in them. Have patience. They're worth waiting for.

You may substitute unbleached white flour for either the whole wheat pastry flour or the brown rice flour.

Count on 30 minutes from start to finish

INGREDIENTS

    1 cup whole wheat pastry flour
½ cup brown rice flour
½ teaspoon salt
½ teaspoon cinnamon
    1 large apple
1 ½ cups water
    2 teaspoons oil

YOU'LL ALSO NEED

    1 bowl (medium)
1 set measuring spoons
1 measuring cup
1 knife
1 wooden cooking spoon
1 peeler
1 corer
1 skillet (10 inches)
1 spatula

WHAT TO DO

1. Mix flours and salt together.
2. Peel and core apple. Slice into small cubes.
3. Slowly mix the water into the flour.
4. Add apple pieces and cinnamon.
5. Pour in enough oil to cover bottom of skillet or griddle. Heat for about 3 minutes. The pan is hot enough when you sprinkle a drop of water on it and it sizzles.
6. Dip the cooking spoon into the pancake batter. Drop the batter into the pan. Cook pancakes on a medium flame. They will need to cook for about 5 minutes on each side because they have no baking soda in them. Turn over when golden brown on the bottom.
7. Serve with honey or pure maple syrup or plain. This makes enough for 4.

FRENCH TOAST

Bread that is a few days old makes great French Toast.

Count on 20 minutes from start to finish

INGREDIENTS

8	slices whole wheat bread
2	eggs
½	cup milk
¼	teaspoon vanilla (optional)
½	teaspoon cinnamon (optional)
½	teaspoon salt
1	chunk butter

YOU'LL ALSO NEED

1	bowl (medium)
1	flat plate
1	measuring cup
1	set measuring spoons
1	skillet (large)
1	fork
1	spatula

WHAT TO DO

1. Crack the eggs against the side of the bowl. Drop the insides of each egg into the bowl. Throw away the shells.
2. Mix in the milk, salt, vanilla, and cinnamon. Beat mixture with a fork until it is well blended.
3. Quickly dip in each slice of bread so that it gets covered

with the egg mixture. Do not let the bread soak in it. Put the slices on a flat plate.

4. Heat the butter in the skillet over a medium flame.

5. Cook as many pieces of bread in the skillet as you can at one time. Each slice should cook until it is golden brown (about 3-4 minutes) on the bottom. Turn each slice over with a spatula.

6. Serves 4. Top with real maple syrup, honey, Apple Sauce Jam (see recipe p. 36), or fresh fruit.

MICHAEL'S SCRAMBLED OMELETTE

My grown-up friend Michael taught me this one. I think of it as a special treat.

Count on 15 minutes from start to finish

INGREDIENTS

2	eggs
2	tablespoons milk
2	slices Muenster cheese
½	teaspoon salt
1	scallion
	pinch rosemary
	pinch thyme
1	chunk butter (small)
1	sprig of parsley (optional)

YOU'LL ALSO NEED

1	bowl (small)
1	cutting board
1	knife
1	set measuring spoons
1	iron skillet (10 inches)
1	fork
1	potholder
1	spatula

WHAT TO DO

1. Wash the scallion. Dice it. Place the pieces in a bowl.
2. Crack the eggs on the side of the bowl. Drop in the eggs. Throw away the shells.

3. Mix in the milk, salt, rosemary, and thyme. Beat mixture
    with a fork.
4. Dice the cheese into small pieces and add to egg mixture.
5. Melt a chunk of butter in a skillet over medium heat.
6. Pour in egg mixture.
7. After the eggs have cooked for about 3 minutes and the
    bottom is firm take a potholder and place pan under the
    broiler until top gets cooked (about 3 minutes).
8. Fold it in half with a spatula. Enough for 1. Serve topped
    with a sprig of parsley.

LUNCH

Lunch is the middle-of-the-day refresher. After a few hours you use up your breakfast energy and your stomach lets you know it is ready for more nourishment by making you feel hungry. Lunch comes at a nice time, too. Right in the middle of the school day.

If you eat lunch in school, you can prepare a sandwich the night before to take with you. If you are at home you just might want to go into the kitchen and make yourself some soup or a salad or a sandwich. These foods are simple and light but will keep you alert and bright.

One nice thing about lunch is that you don't need to eat a huge meal to keep your body motor running. Remember, it is the quality rather than the quantity of the food you eat that really counts.

HARRIET'S MELTED CHEESE SANDWICH

Count on 10 minutes from start to finish

INGREDIENTS

    2 slices whole wheat bread
    2 slices Muenster, Swiss, or Monterey Jack cheese
    2 pinches of thyme

YOU'LL ALSO NEED

       a broiler or a toaster oven
    1 knife
    1 potholder

WHAT TO DO

1. Place cheese slices on bread.
2. Sprinkle each slice with pinch of thyme. Turn stove to broil.
3. Put slices under broiler and let them cook until the cheese is melted (about 5 minutes). Be careful taking the sandwich out of the oven. It is hot.
4. Makes a mouth-tickling lunch or snack. Serve it alone or with a salad or soup. Enough for just you. If you're making lunch for family or friends count on 2 extra slices for each guest.

EGG DROP SOUP

Here's a Chinese soup that you can prepare with the toss of a chopstick. The trick is the stock. Use water left over from cooking vegetables. An especially good stock comes from soaking Chinese dried mushrooms. So if you live near a good health food store or a place that sells Chinese products you're in business. Here's what you do. Place about 10 Chinese mushrooms in a large bowl. Pour enough boiling water over the mushrooms to fill ¾ of the bowl. Let it stand for 15-20 minutes. Use the water as stock and the mushrooms in almost any vegetable dish. If you have no stock of any kind, use 1 can of chicken broth. But only as a last resort.

Takes 15 minutes from start to finish

INGREDIENTS

- 4 cups stock
- 1 tablespoon arrowroot
- 1 cup water
- 1 teaspoon salt
- 1 egg
- 3 scallions

YOU'LL ALSO NEED

- 1 pot (medium)
- 1 bowl (small)
- 1 fork
- 1 wooden chopstick
- 1 knife
- 1 set measuring spoons
- 1 measuring cup

WHAT TO DO

1. Put stock or broth into the pot. Place it over medium high heat.
2. Dissolve the arrowroot in the cup of water. Mix it well.

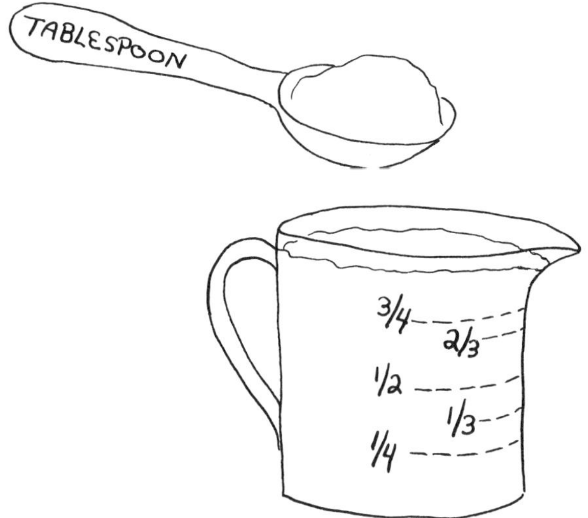

3. When the stock is simmering, stir in arrowroot mixture and salt.
4. After the stock has boiled for about 1 minute, turn the heat off.
5. Crack the egg into the bowl. Beat it well with a fork.
6. Slowly pour the egg into the hot stock and stir it around with a chopstick.
7. Wash and dice the scallions. Add several pieces to each bowl of soup before serving. Serves 4.

PEANUT BUTTER

The best peanut butter is the kind you make yourself. Use either raw or roasted peanuts. I like to use raw nuts because they're better for you, but you're probably used to the roasted kind. Buy them in the shell or out of the shell, depending on how lazy you are. You also need a blender for this one. It's a real mouth-smacker.

Count on 20 minutes from start to finish

INGREDIENTS

    1 pound raw or roasted peanuts
½ teaspoon salt (optional)
    1 or 2 tablespoons corn or sesame oil (The more oil you use, the creamier it will be.)

YOU'LL ALSO NEED

1 empty pint-size jar with cover
1 blender
1 set measuring spoons

WHAT TO DO

If your blender is small or has only a few speeds, you may have to make this in 2 or 3 batches.

1. Place shelled peanuts in the blender.
2. Add salt if you like your peanut butter salted.
3. Add 1 teaspoon oil. Place cover on blender. Start it at a low speed. When peanuts are ground up into small pieces, put blender on a higher speed.

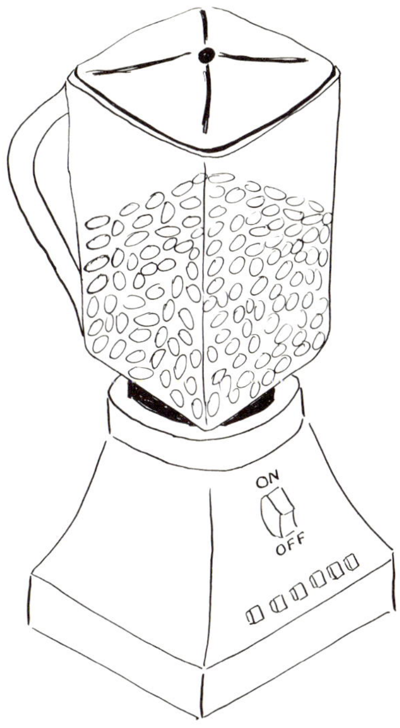

4. To make peanut butter creamier, stop the blender and add more oil. If you'd like it saltier, add more salt. Put top on again and set speed at low. After a few minutes, raise speed to high.

5. It should take from 5 to 10 minutes to grind each batch of peanuts. This depends on how powerful your blender is.

6. Take the peanut butter out of the blender. Before you eat it all, put it in a jar that closes tightly. You may store it in the refrigerator. It helps to keep it fresh. This amount should fit into a pint-size jar. The longer the peanut butter stands, the thicker it will get.

PEANUT BUTTER SANDWICH IDEAS

1. Make your peanut butter into lunch by smearing it on whole wheat bread along with a layer of Apple Sauce Jam (see recipe p. 36) or apple butter.
2. Spread peanut butter on whole grain bread. Top it with very ripe banana slices.
3. Smear peanut butter on a slice of whole grain bread. Smooth on a layer of honey.

Another sandwich idea is to leave out the peanut butter and spread a layer of Apple Sauce Jam on a slice of whole grain bread. Spread the other slice of bread with cream cheese. Put them together and bite in.

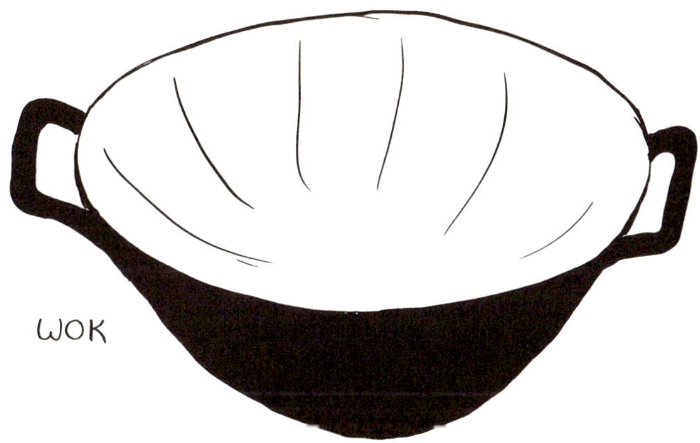

VEGETABLE FRIED RICE

Cut up each vegetable while the one you've just cut is heating up. Stir after adding each one. You may substitute other vegetables such as zucchini, onions, or carrots for the ones listed.

Count on 30 minutes from start to finish

INGREDIENTS

    2 cups cooked brown rice (see recipe p. 70)
    3 scallions
    1 green pepper (medium)
    2 stalks celery
    2 stalks broccoli
    2 cloves garlic
    1 small piece ginger or ½ teaspoon powdered
        ginger
    1 tablespoon peanut or corn oil
    1 tablespoon tamari

    1 Chinese chopstick or fork
    1 cutting board
    1 grater
    1 skillet (large) or wok
    1 knife
    1 garlic press
    1 peeler

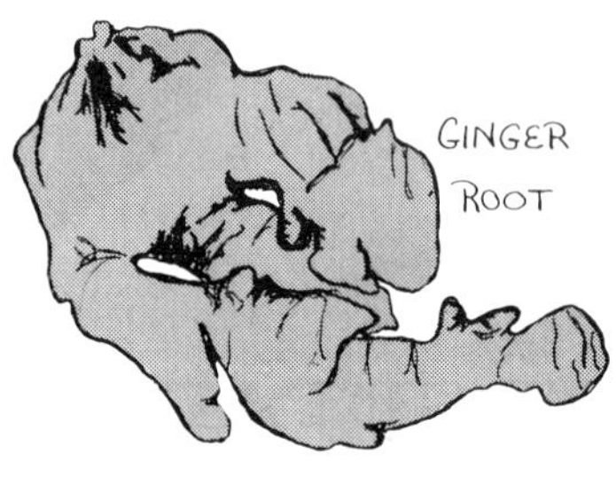

WHAT TO DO

1. Wash vegetables. Dice scallions. Throw away white stringy tips. Separate the green top parts of the scallions from the bottom white parts.

2. Heat oil in the skillet or wok on a high flame until it sizzles a little (about 3 minutes).

3. Add white pieces of diced scallions. Turn flame to low. Let scallions cook for about 2 minutes.

4. Dice green pepper. Add to scallions in the skillet.

5. Dice celery. Add to other vegetables after green pepper has cooked for about 2 minutes.

6. Dice broccoli. Add to vegetables after celery has cooked for about 2 minutes.

7. Add green tops of scallions to vegetables after broccoli has cooked for about 5 minutes. Let them heat for 1 minute. Then add rice.

8. Peel the garlic. Put it in the garlic press and squeeze the garlic over the vegetables and rice. If you don't have a

54

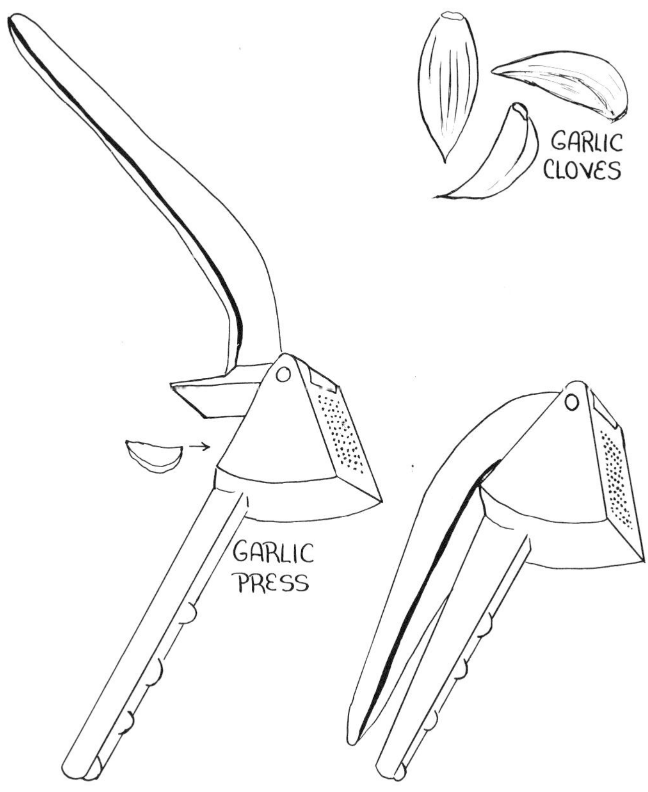

crusher, cut the garlic into very tiny pieces. Add the pieces to the vegetables and rice. Stir.

9. Peel off the brown skin of the ginger. Grate the ginger by rubbing it up and down on the grater. Add grated or powered ginger to the vegetables and rice. Stir.

10. Sprinkle the tamari over rice and vegetables. Stir.

11. Cook rice and vegetables uncovered for about 10-15 minutes longer on medium flame.

12. Serve topped with a sprig of parsley or with sesame salt. Makes enough for 4.

TOASTED TUNA SANDWICH

I don't ordinarily like to use cans of food but this is so delicious, consider it an exception.

Takes 15 minutes from start to finish

INGREDIENTS

1 large can tuna fish (7 ounces)
1 onion (medium)
2 tablespoons mayonnaise
1 small green pepper
  pinch of thyme (optional)
8 small slices of Muenster cheese
4 tablespoons bean sprouts (optional)
4 English muffins

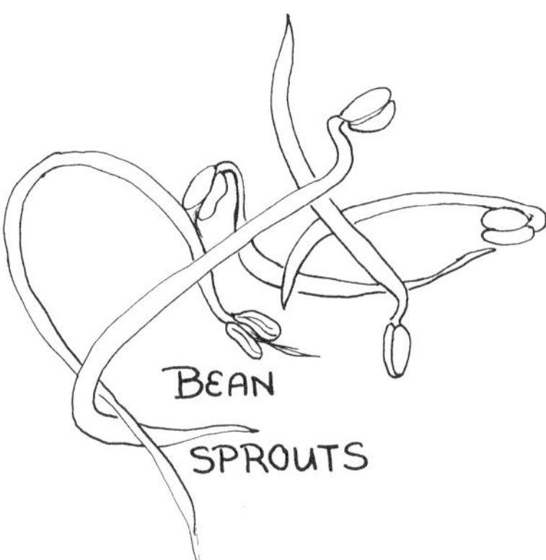

YOU'LL ALSO NEED

1 bowl (medium)
1 fork
1 knife
1 set measuring spoons
1 cutting board
1 potholder

56

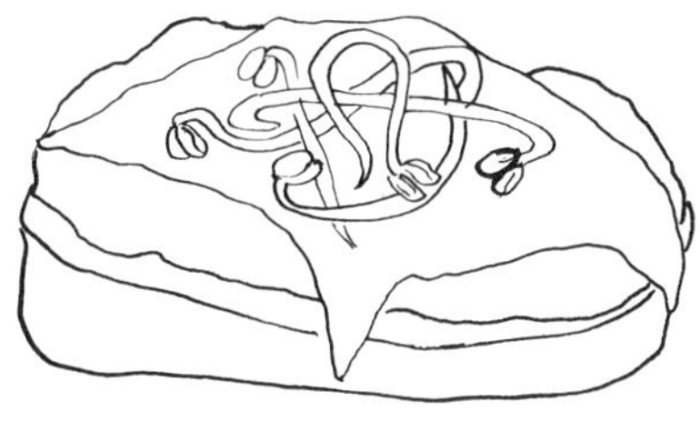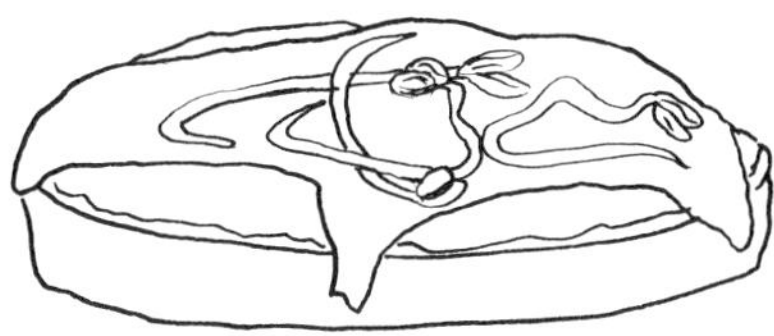

WHAT TO DO

1. Place the tuna fish in the bowl. Add the mayonnaise. Mash both together with a fork.
2. Peel and dice the onion. Mix in well with tuna fish. Add the thyme.
3. Wash and cut green pepper into strips.
4. Pile a scoop of tuna fish on each English muffin half.
5. Place a strip of green pepper and a slice of cheese on top of each half.
6. Toast under broiler until cheese melts (about 4 minutes).
7. Use potholder to remove from oven. Sprinkle on bean sprouts. Serve each person two halves.

VEGETABLE PANCAKES

Here's some advice to the fancy chef. Flip pancakes at your own risk. If you miss you might wind up washing the kitchen floor as well as the dishes.

Count on 30 minutes from start to finish

INGREDIENTS

        1 ½   cups whole wheat pastry flour
          1   tablespoon arrowroot
          ½   teaspoon salt
          1   onion (medium)
          1   carrot (medium)
        1 ½   cups water
          1   tablespoon oil

YOU'LL ALSO NEED

          1   cutting board
          1   knife
          1   scrub brush for vegetables
          1   bowl (medium)
          1   skillet (10 inches)
          1   measuring cup
          1   set measuring spoons
          1   wooden spoon
          1   spatula

WHAT TO DO

1. Peel onion. Wash it. Cut it in half lengthwise and place flat side on board. Close your fingers to the knuckle on your left hand if you are a rightie and the other way

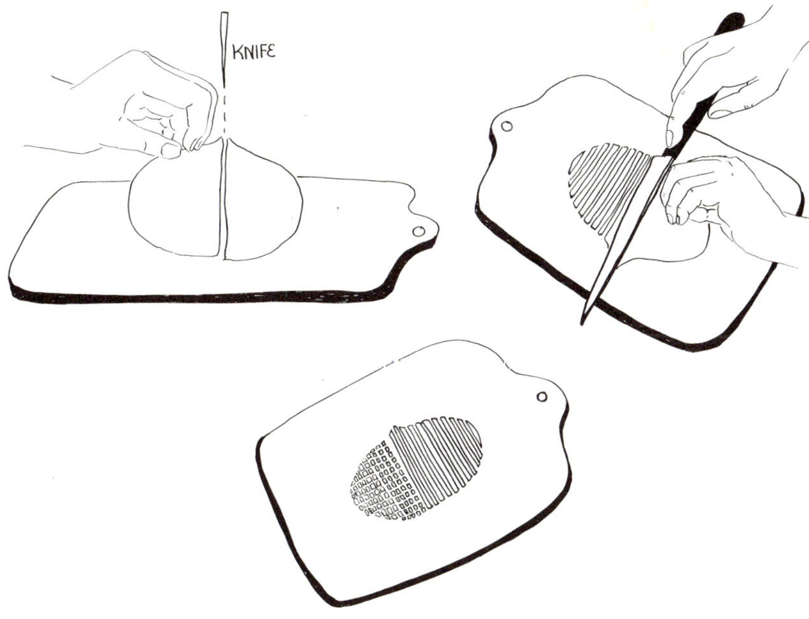

around if you are a leftie. Take the knife in your other hand. Place your hand with the closed fingers on top of the onion. Begin to slice the onion. Your fingers should act as a guide for the knife by moving back as the knife moves forward. When you've sliced about half the onion, turn it on its other end and begin to slice it from the other side.

2. Dice the onion by placing the slices flat and slicing them across both ways.

3. Wash carrot with scrub brush. Place it on the cutting board and cut off the tip of the pointed side and the very top of the carrot. Slice the carrot on a slant in ¼-inch pieces from the pointed end to the top. Put 2 or 3 slices

59

on top of each other. Cut the slices in half lengthwise
and then across. Do this with all the carrot slices. You now
have diced carrots.

4. Mix all the ingredients except the oil in a bowl. Place
   them in the bowl in the order in which they're listed.

5. Heat oil on medium flame in a skillet or on a griddle. Use
   a spoon to drop the batter into the pan. Make the pancakes as large or small as you like.

6. Let the pancakes get brown on the bottom side (5
   minutes). Then turn them over with a spatula. Let pancakes brown on the other side (about 5 minutes).

7. Makes about 8 pancakes. Serve with tamari for a luncheon
   treat with a Japanese flavor.

BIG BOWL SALAD

*Count on 15 minutes from start to finish, plus a few
more minutes for the dressing*

INGREDIENTS

    1 small head Romaine lettuce
    1 small cucumber
    1 small green pepper
    1 or 2 slices Muenster cheese
       handful of bean sprouts (optional)

YOU'LL ALSO NEED

    1 cutting board
    1 knife
    1 bowl (large)
    1 peeler
    1 wooden spoon

WHAT TO DO

1. Separate the lettuce leaves and wash them. Tear or cut each leaf into bite-size pieces. Place them in a bowl.
2. Wash green pepper. Take out the core. Cut the pepper into 4 sections. Dice each section. Place pieces in the bowl.
3. Peel cucumber. Slice it. Dice it. Put it in the bowl.
4. Cut cheese into bite-size pieces. Put pieces in the bowl. Add the bean sprouts. Mix all the vegetables together.
5. Serve with Sesame Salt (see recipe p. 109) or Sesame Tamari Dressing (see recipe p. 63) or a mixture of 2 tablespoons vegetable oil plus 1 teaspoon salt. If you make a dressing, pour it over the salad. Dig in. Serves 4.

SESAME TAMARI DRESSING

Count on 10 minutes from start to finish

INGREDIENTS

    ¼ cup sesame or peanut or corn oil
    ¼ cup tamari
    1 slice of lemon

YOU'LL ALSO NEED

    1 bowl (small)
    1 measuring cup
    1 spoon

WHAT TO DO

1. Pour oil and tamari into the bowl. Mix it with a lot of energy and a spoon for about 3 minutes.
2. Squeeze the slice of lemon into the mixture.
3. Pour over any salad. Goes especially well with the Big Bowl Salad (see recipe p. 61). Serves 4.

DINNER

Dinner has always been my favorite meal. I like it because it's the meal that brings people together after a day which everyone has spent in a different way.

I also like the food served at dinner. When I was growing up I thought that dinner had to be a piece of meat or fish or chicken and a potato and vegetable. What a nice surprise to find out there are so many more choices than that. For instance, your whole meal can be made up of different kinds of vegetables and grains. This kind of meal gives you lots of vitamins and leaves you feeling light and bouncy instead of like a 50-pound barbell.

There are many different kinds of well-balanced meals. One good one is a soup or salad followed by a combination of vegetables, maybe some beans, and a grain. After the main course, you may want some dessert or a beverage.

To balance a meal means to use foods that give you the combination of vitamins and minerals you need to feel good. Different foods offer you different nutrients. It is a good idea to put together foods that complement or complete one another. For example, if you were making a combination of vegetables, you wouldn't cook three green vegetables. Instead, you might try one white vegetable, like an onion, and one green vegetable, like broccoli, and one orange vegetable, like a carrot. Each of these foods has different vitamins to offer. Sometimes the colors or shapes of foods help us to see their nutritional differences.

To plan a well-balanced meal, combine a clear head, lots of time, and good food.

66

SAUTÉED CHICKEN WITH MUSHROOMS

Goes great over brown rice.

Count on 30 minutes cooking time, plus 1 hour soaking time

INGREDIENTS

A. for sauce to soak the chicken
enough tamari to cover chicken
1 clove garlic

B. for dish
4 boneless chicken breasts
1 onion (medium)
2 teaspoons vegetable oil
1 pint or ¾ pound fresh mushrooms
1 green pepper (medium)
1 clove garlic
1 teaspoon powdered ginger
1 teaspoon salt
4 sprigs parsley

YOU'LL ALSO NEED
1 skillet (large)
1 knife
1 set measuring spoons
1 bowl (large)
1 garlic press (optional)
1 cutting board

WHAT TO DO

To Soak the Chicken

1. Wash the chicken pieces. Cut them into bite-size pieces. Put them in a bowl.
2. Peel the clove of garlic. Either chop it into small pieces or crush it in a garlic press.
3. Put the garlic pieces or crushed garlic on the chicken pieces. Pour enough tamari over the pieces to cover them. Let the chicken stay in the refrigerator for an hour. Remove it 20 minutes before starting to cook it.

To Sauté

1. Peel the other garlic clove. Chop it into tiny pieces or squeeze it in a garlic press. (If you use a garlic press, wait until the oil is heated. Then squeeze garlic directly into the skillet.)
2. Peel onion and wash it. Dice it into medium-size pieces.
3. Place oil in skillet. Heat on medium flame for 2 minutes. Put flame on low. Add garlic. Sauté the onion until you can see through it (about 3 minutes).
4. While the onion is sautéing, wash the green pepper. Cut around the core of the pepper.
5. Take the chicken out of the bowl. Rub salt and ginger on both sides of the chicken pieces.
6. Put the chicken into the skillet.
7. Wash the mushrooms.
8. Slice the mushrooms lengthwise (long way across). Each

68

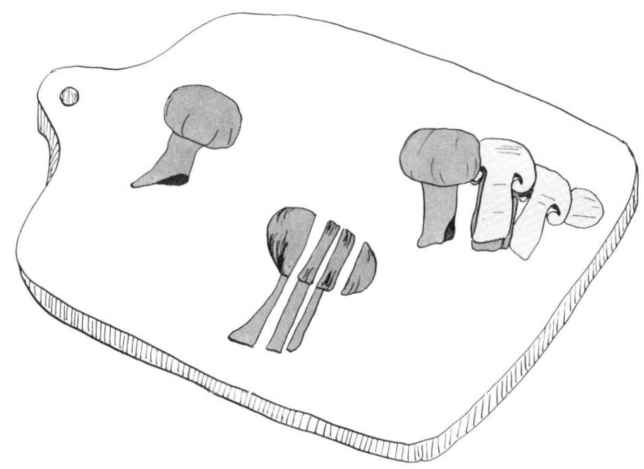

mushroom should be cut into 3 or 4 pieces. Add to chicken and onions. Stir.

9. Pour about 1 cup of the tamari left over from soaking the chicken over the mixture.

10. Cook for 10 or 15 minutes on medium-low flame until the pink chicken turns white. Stir occasionally.

11. This dish goes especially well served over rice or noodles. To add the finishing touch, wash 4 sprigs of parsley and place on top of each serving. Enough for 4.

BROWN RICE

Brown rice is a basic food that goes well with just about anything. Count on ½ cup dry rice per person when you're trying to figure out how much to make. It's always a good idea to make extra rice. You can use it in the Vegetable Fried Rice recipe.

Count on 1 hour from start to finish

INGREDIENTS

    2 cups brown rice (short or long grain)
    4 cups water
    1 teaspoon sea salt
      sprinkling tamari or pinch of herbs (optional)

YOU'LL ALSO NEED

    1 pot with cover (medium)
    1 set measuring spoons
    1 measuring cup
    1 strainer (optional)
    1 wooden chopstick or fork

WHAT TO DO

1. Measure out 2 cups of rice.
2. Put the rice into the pot.
3. Wash the rice carefully. There are two ways you can wash the rice. One is to fill the pot halfway with water and stir the rice around with a chopstick or fork. The water will become cloudy. Spill the water out of the pot by covering the pot and leaving a small opening for the water to

spill out. The other way is to fill the pot halfway with water. Stir the rice and pour it into a strainer. The water will spill out of the strainer through the holes. Whichever method you use, wash the rice at least three times or until the water is clear.

4. When the rice is clean, place it in a pot and add 4 cups of water to it, and herbs if you are using them. Place the pot over a high flame and wait until the water boils.

5. When it boils, turn the flame to low. Add the salt, cover the pot, and let it simmer for 45 minutes. Check occasionally to make sure it is cooking slowly. If you want to add a special flavor to it, sprinkle a few drops of tamari soy sauce over the rice about 10 minutes before it is finished cooking.

6. This makes enough for 4, with some left over for seconds.

FRESH CLAM SAUCE

Count on 30 minutes from start to finish

INGREDIENTS

1 dozen fresh clams
2 cloves garlic
2 cups clam juice saved from cooking clams
3 sprigs parsley
½ teaspoon salt
pinch thyme
2 tablespoons sesame or corn oil

YOU'LL ALSO NEED

1 pot (large) with steamer tray or 1 fish
   poacher pot
1 scrub brush for clams
1 pot (small)
1 pot (medium)
1 cutting board
1 knife

WHAT TO DO

1. Wash and scrub clams well because there may be sand in them.
2. Place about 2 inches water in the bottom of the pot you will use to steam clams. Heat it on high flame until it boils. Put steamer tray into the pot. Place clams on tray and

lower flame to medium so that water simmers. Cover.

3. Cook clams until the shells open up—about 15 minutes. After clam shells open up, remove from pot and take out the clam meat with a fork. Be sure to save the liquid left over from cooking the clams. This is the clam juice. But if there are particles of sand at the bottom of the liquid, pour off the top part of the clear clam juice and save it. Throw away the liquid with the sand particles in it.

4. In a small pot heat 2 tablespoons oil. Peel cloves of garlic. Cut them in pieces so tiny you can hardly see them. This is called mincing. Heat the oil for about 3 minutes over a medium flame. Add the garlic pieces.

5. Slowly add 2 cups of clam juice to the garlic. Wash the sprigs of parsley and chop them up into small pieces. Add the parsley, salt, and thyme to the mixture. Cover and simmer for 15 minutes.

6. Chop up the clam meat into small pieces. Add it to the mixture that is cooking. Cook mixture for another 3 minutes, just long enough to heat up the clams.

7. Serve over whole wheat spaghetti or noodles. Serves 4.

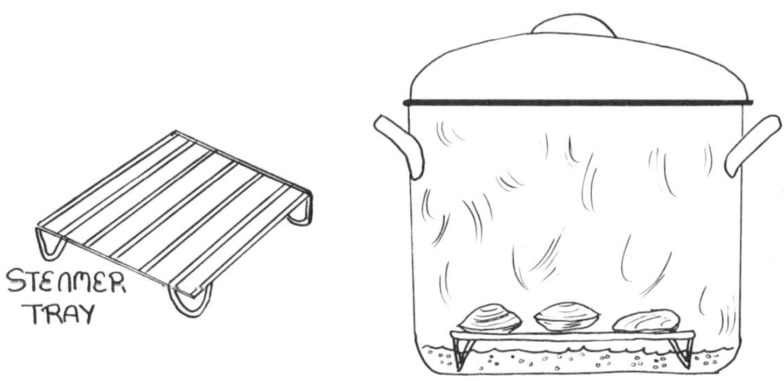

WHOLE WHEAT SPAGHETTI OR NOODLES

This is just plain old spaghetti that happens to be good for you, too. Here's the Japanese way to make them. It keeps them firm. (They are called either spaghetti or noodles.)

Takes 20 minutes from start to finish

INGREDIENTS

1	pound whole wheat spaghetti or noodles
½	potful of water
½	cup tamari (optional)
1 ½	cups cold water

YOU'LL ALSO NEED

1	pot with cover (large)
1	measuring cup
1	colander or strainer
1	potholder
1	large bowl (optional)

WHAT TO DO

1. Fill the pot half full of water. Place it over a high flame until it boils.
2. Add the spaghetti or noodles. Lower flame to medium.
3. When the water boils again add ½ cup cold water. When it boils again add another ½ cup cold water. Do this 3 times all together. Each time you add the cold water, the spaghetti water will stop boiling. Wait until the water boils again after you've added the last ½ cup of water.

Turn the flame off. Cover the pot. Let it sit for 2 minutes.

4. Using a potholder, carefully carry the spaghetti pot to the sink. Pour the spaghetti and spaghetti water into a colander or strainer. If you want to save the spaghetti water, place a bowl under the colander. It is good water to use when cooking soups or sauces or making breads. Place the spaghetti water in the refrigerator, covered. It will keep for about a week.

5. If you're serving the spaghetti plain, add tamari to it for flavoring. Or add your own sauce, like Fresh Clam Sauce (see recipe p. 72).

6. This recipe makes enough for 4.

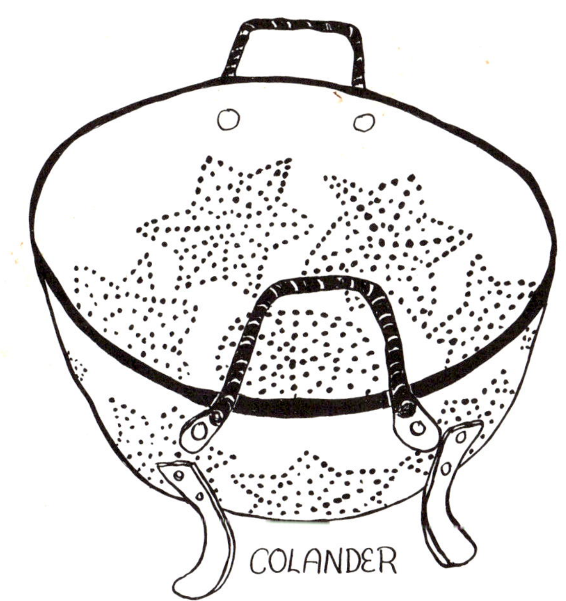

SQUASH STUFFED WITH BULGHUR

Count on 1 hour and 15 minutes from start to finish

INGREDIENTS

- 1 ½ cups bulghur wheat
- 3 cups water
- 1 carrot (medium)
- 1 onion (medium)
- 1 teaspoon salt
- 3 teaspoons corn oil
- 2 acorn squash (medium)

FOR SAUCE

- 2 cloves garlic
- 3 tablespoons corn oil
- 3 tablespoons tamari
- 1 tablespoon sesame seeds

YOU'LL ALSO NEED

- 1 measuring cup
- 1 set measuring spoons
- 1 pastry brush or 1 paper towel
- 2 pots (small, 1 with cover)
- 1 Pyrex pie plate (11 inches)
- 1 wooden chopstick or fork
- 1 knife
- 1 scrub brush for vegetables
- 1 dish (small)
- 1 potholder
- 1 garlic press (optional)

WHAT TO DO

1. Preheat oven to 425° F. Cut both squash in half lengthwise. Remove the seeds. (You may save them and roast them. See recipe for Roasted Seeds p. 103.)

2. Pour ½ teaspoon corn oil on each piece of squash. Spread it around with a pastry brush or paper towel. Put squash in pie plate and bake at 425° for 45 minutes.

3. In a separate pot, boil 3 cups of water.

4. Peel, wash, and dice onion into small pieces.

5. In a pot, heat 1 teaspoon corn oil on high flame for 2 minutes. Turn flame to low. Add diced onion.

6. Cook onion until it is clear—about 3 minutes. Then add bulghur. Stir onion and bulghur with a chopstick or fork so that it cooks evenly. Let bulghur sauté for about 3 minutes.

7. Wash and scrub carrot. Then dice it into small pieces. Add to bulghur and stir. Sauté for 2 minutes.

8. Using a potholder, pour boiling water over bulghur slowly and carefully. Add salt. Cover. Cook on a low flame until water disappears (about 15 minutes). Check occasionally.

9. To make sauce, mix oil and tamari together. Peel garlic. Crush garlic cloves with a garlic press or cut them into very tiny pieces. Add the garlic to the oil and tamari. Then mix in the sesame seeds.

10. Take the squash out of the oven. Stuff the scooped-out parts of both squash with the bulghur mixture. Pour the sauce over the squash and bulghur. Cook the stuffed squash in the oven for an additional 15-20 minutes.

11. Serves 4. Use the leftover bulghur as a side dish.

SIMPLE SALAD

This salad only takes a few minutes to prepare and goes well with all the recipes in the Dinner section. It makes you think that Popeye was right all along about spinach.

Takes 15 minutes from start to finish

INGREDIENTS

1 package or 1 pound of fresh spinach leaves
1 pint or ¾ pound fresh mushrooms
2 scallions

YOU'LL ALSO NEED

    1 mixing bowl (large)
    1 knife
    1 cutting board
    1 salad bowl (optional)
    5 or 6 paper towels
    2 clean hands

WHAT TO DO

1. Wash the spinach leaves carefully. Wrap them up in paper towels to dry them. Put them in the refrigerator or another cool place.
2. Carefully wash each mushroom. Slice each one lengthwise (the long way) into about 4 pieces. Place in mixing bowl.
3. Wash the scallions. Cut off the stringy white tip. Dice the scallions into small pieces. Place them in the mixing bowl.
4. Take the spinach leaves out of the paper towels. Tear each leaf into small pieces. Place them in the mixing bowl.
5. Mix the mushrooms, scallions, and spinach together. Do this with a fork or two clean hands.
6. Serves 4. Goes well with Sesame Tamari Dressing (see recipe p. 63).

FISH

There is a whole oceanful of fish you can choose from to prepare a tasty and healthy meal. Some of the ones I like best are haddock, halibut, filet of sole, scallops, swordfish, and shrimp. You can cook fish by broiling, boiling, baking, poaching, or by cooking it on top of the stove (pan frying). To find out the differences between all these ways of cooking, check the glossary. Try this recipe either broiled or baked. If you decide to bake, preheat the oven to 350° about 15 minutes before you're ready to cook the fish.

Count on 1 hour to marinate, plus 15 minutes to cook fish

80

INGREDIENTS

>   4 pieces or 1¾ to 2 pounds of haddock,
>   halibut, filet of sole, or swordfish
> ½ cup tamari
> ¼ cup water
>   1 small piece of ginger
>   4 sprigs parsley

YOU'LL ALSO NEED

>   1 peeler
>   1 Pyrex pie plate (11 inches) or broiler pan or
>   baking dish
>   1 small bowl or cup
>   1 fork
>   1 grater (optional)

WHAT TO DO

1. Place the 4 pieces of fish in the pan or baking dish. In a separate cup or bowl, mix the tamari with the water. Then peel the piece of ginger. Grate the ginger into the tamari.

2. Pour the tamari mixture over the fish. Let the fish soak or marinate for 30 minutes. Then turn it over and let it soak for another 30 minutes.

3. Broil the fish or bake it at 350° F. for about 7 minutes on each side or until it feels flaky when you prick it with a fork.

4. Enough for 4. Top each piece with a sprig of parsley. Serve with a grain like rice or bulghur, and a vegetable.

DESSERTS

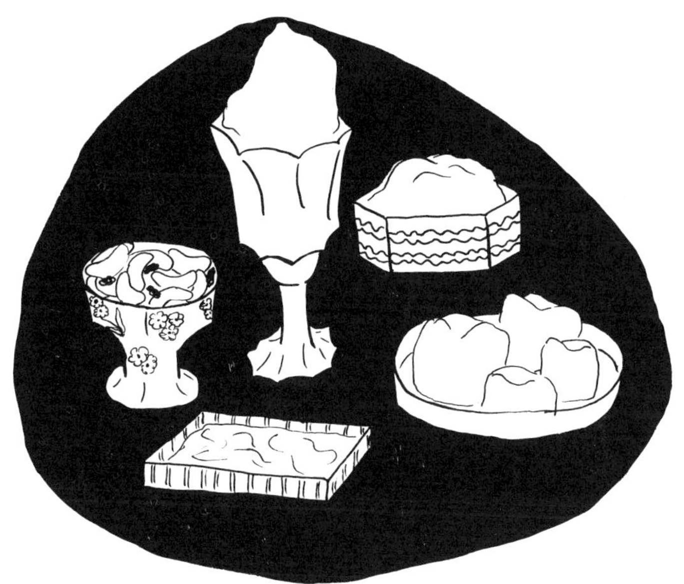

THE LOWDOWN ON SUGAR

I have some sad news for you. But don't worry. I have some happy news for you, too. The sad news is that sugar is bad for you. It has no vitamins or minerals and helps to dig cavities into your teeth.

White sugar is not good for you. Neither is brown sugar. Brown sugar is really just white sugar with some molasses added to it. Now, molasses is a good food to eat because it has B vitamins and iron. But, we can do without the sugar part.

The same sad tale is true of "raw" or turbinado sugar. This sugar is almost as bad as white sugar. The difference is that "raw sugar" goes through one less refining process than white sugar.

Now that I've told you all the sad news, get ready for the happy part. I know most of you like to eat sweet things. There is a way to make sweet desserts that are also good for you, too. Best of all, it's simple as apple pie.

There are foods you can use instead of sugar. Honey is one of them. It is sweet. You can use it in desserts. And it is better for you than sugar. Some of the recipes in this section are made with honey.

There's also another way to make sweet desserts. You can

use dried fruits like raisins, currants, apricots, or other fruits. You can also cook with drinks that are sweet, like apple juice. The good thing about fruits is that they are naturally sweet. They grow with sugar already inside them.

I hope you have stopped worrying by now. You can make desserts taste good and be good for you at the same time. The recipes on the following pages will help you fill up that "sweet tooth" without making cavities in it.

HOW TO CORE AN APPLE

To core means to take out the hard center part of the apple that contains the seeds. This part is not good to eat.

The fastest and easiest way to do this is to use a corer that has a pointed tip.

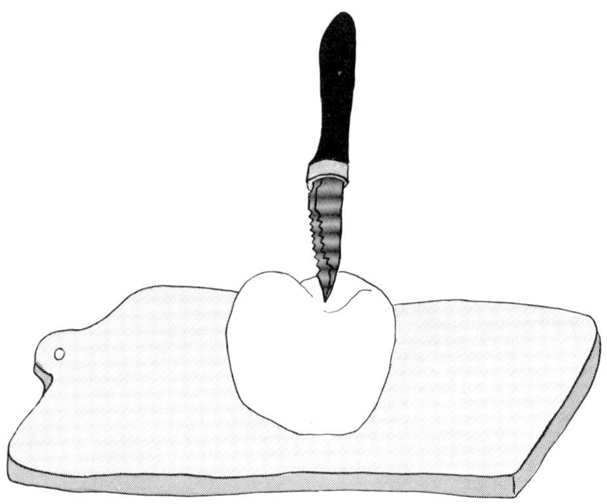

WHAT TO DO

Put the apple on the cutting board. Press the tip of the corer into the top of the apple near the stem. Push the corer into the apple. Turn it until it gets to the bottom end. If you are making baked apples, stop before you go through the other end. For all other apples, go through the other end. Then remove the core.

Now you are ready to slice the apple.

HOW TO OIL A PAN

YOU'LL NEED

> 1 plate or pan or dish
> 1 pastry brush or square of paper towel
> 1 teaspoon oil

Sometimes you need to oil a pan or dish before you cook in it, to keep food from sticking to it. The oil is slippery and coats the dish.

WHAT TO DO

Pour the oil into pan. Use a pastry brush or piece of paper towel to spread the oil all over the pan. It's just like painting. Only this time, you're using a pastry brush and pan instead of a paint brush and paper. Remember to cover the whole bottom of the pan and the sides, too. This will help the food to come out of the pan easily after it is cooked.

APPLE BROWN BETTY DELIGHT

This recipe may look hard to make but it's really easy. I think you'll like the taste.

Count on 30 minutes to prepare, plus 1 hour baking time

INGREDIENTS

            5 cooking apples
            1 wedge lemon (medium)
            2 cups whole wheat bread crumbs
            3 tablespoons sunflower seeds or nuts
            3 tablespoons raisins
           ½ cup unsweetened apple juice
           ¼ cup honey
            1 teaspoon cinnamon
            1 teaspoon corn oil

YOU'LL ALSO NEED

            1 corer
            1 Pyrex ovenware dish or casserole dish
                 (about 2 quarts)
            1 pastry brush or paper towel
            1 cutting board
            1 bowl (medium)
            1 knife

WHAT TO DO

1. Preheat oven to 350° F.
2. Wash the apples. Peel them if you wish, but it's not

necessary. Core and slice them into bite-size wedges about ½ inch wide.

3. Oil the baking dish.

4. This dessert is made in layers. The first layer is made up of apples. Put about half the apple pieces in the bottom of the baking dish.

5. Cut the soft part of the lemon (the part that squirts when you squeeze it) away from the rind (the hard part). Cut the rind into tiny pieces (about as large as the nail on your pinky). Put half the cut slices in between the apple slices.

6. Take 3 slices of whole wheat bread and crumble them into small pieces (about as large as your thumbnail). Use as many slices as you need to make 2 cups of bread crumbs. Take 1 cup of those crumbs and sprinkle them over the apples. Then sprinkle 1½ tablespoons of the raisins and 1½ tablespoons of the seeds or nuts over the bread crumbs.

7. Make the same layers listed in directions 4, 5, 6, again— apple slices, lemon rind, bread crumbs, raisins, and seeds or nuts and place them on top of the first layer.

8. In a separate small bowl, mix the honey, apple juice, and cinnamon together. Pour this over the layers in the baking dish.

9. Bake in a 350° F. oven for an hour.

10. When you take the dessert out of the oven, let it cool for about 10 minutes. Then mix the layers together with a spoon before serving it. You will have enough for 4 large portions with enough left over for seconds.

BAKED APPLES

Count on 50 minutes from start to finish

INGREDIENTS

       4 cooking apples
       4 tablespoons raisins or currants
       4 tablespoons honey
       1 teaspoon cinnamon

YOU'LL ALSO NEED

       1 baking dish or baking tray (medium)
       1 apple corer
       1 set measuring spoons

WHAT TO DO

1. Preheat oven to 375° F.
2. Wash and core the apples. Be careful not to scoop out the bottoms of the apples.
3. Fill the centers of the apples with currants or raisins.
4. Put the apples in the baking tray or dish.
5. Mix the cinnamon into the honey. Pour honey over each apple.
6. Bake apples for 40 minutes. Serves 4. Great winter dessert.

ORANGE DELICIOUS

Count on 20 minutes from start to finish

INGREDIENTS

      4 oranges
     ¼ cup honey
     ⅓ cup water
      1 teaspoon cinnamon
      4 tablespoons unsweetened shredded coconut
      4 tablespoons raisins
         pinch of fresh or dried mint (optional)

YOU'LL ALSO NEED

      1 set measuring spoons
      1 measuring cup
      1 knife
      1 pot (medium) with cover

WHAT TO DO

1. Peel oranges. Separate the sections. Cut each section into small pieces.
2. Mix the honey and water together in the pot. Place pot over medium heat for 3 minutes.
3. Add orange slices, coconut, cinnamon, and raisins to the pot.
4. Cover pot and cook for 10 minutes over medium heat.
5. Top each serving with a pinch of mint. This is a quick dessert. Enough for 4.

FRESHEST FRUIT SALAD

This takes a few different kinds of fresh fruit but no cooking.

Count on 20 minutes from start to finish

INGREDIENTS

    3 peaches
    ¼ cantaloupe
    2 apples
    ½ cup blueberries
    ¼ cup strawberries
    3 tablespoons cherries
    2 tablespoons raisins

YOU'LL ALSO NEED

    1 knife
    1 cutting board
    1 measuring cup
    1 set measuring spoons
    1 bowl (large)
    1 wooden spoon

WHAT TO DO

1. Wash the peaches. Cut the peach away from the peach pit on four sides. Cut each piece of peach into thin slices. Dice it into bite-size pieces. Put pieces in a bowl.

2. Cut the orange part of the cantaloupe away from the rind. Do this by cutting across the bottom where the orange part begins. Cut the cantaloupe into slices. Dice the slices into bite-size pieces. Put the pieces in the bowl.

3. Wash the apples and core them. Slice them thinly. Then dice them into bite-size pieces. Place in bowl.
4. Wash the blueberries. Add them to the other fruits in the bowl.
5. Wash the strawberries. Pull off the green tops. Slice each strawberry into 4 small pieces. Add to bowl.
6. Wash cherries. Take the pits out of them. Add to other fruits.
7. Mix in raisins.
8. Mix all fruits together. Place in dessert dishes. Makes a cool and refreshing warm weather treat for 6 people.

FRUIT FRUITY

You can experiment with this Fruity by trying it with different fruits like dried cherries and tiny pieces of lemon rind.

Count on 25 minutes from start to finish

INGREDIENTS

    4 apples (yellow if possible)
    8 dried apricots
    2 tablespoons raisins
  ½ cup water
    1 teaspoon honey
    8 hazelnuts, peanuts, or cashews

YOU'LL ALSO NEED

    1 peeler (optional)
    1 apple corer
    1 knife
    1 set measuring spoons
    1 measuring cup
    1 cutting board
    1 pot (medium)

WHAT TO DO

1. Wash the apples and core them. It's not necessary to peel them.
2. Dice the apples into small pieces about ¼ inch square.
3. Dice the apricots into small pieces about ¼ inch square.
4. Place water and honey in a pot. Mix them together. Heat for about 5 minutes over medium heat.

94

5. Add apples, apricots, and raisins.

6. Cook for 15 minutes over medium heat, stirring every once in a while. Place in dessert dishes.

7. Chop up nuts into small pieces. Sprinkle a few over each dish. Serves 4.

STRAWBERRY JELLO

I prefer to make jello with agar agar because it is a vegetable product that comes from seaweed. You can find agar agar in a health food store. In place of agar agar you can use un-flavored gelatine. See directions B for the gelatine recipe.

Count on 20 minutes to prepare, plus 1 hour to chill jello

A. INGREDIENTS

- 2¾ cups unsweetened apple juice
- 1 stick agar agar
- ½ pint or about 15 strawberries
- 3 tablespoons raisins or currants (optional)
- pinch of dry or fresh mint

YOU'LL ALSO NEED

- 1 pot (medium)
- 1 bowl to chill and serve jello
- 1 knife
- 1 measuring cup
- 1 set measuring spoons
- 1 wooden chopstick or spoon

WHAT TO DO

1. Rinse the stick of agar agar under cold water. Tear it into 4 or 5 pieces.
2. Pour the apple juice into the pot. Heat it for about 5 minutes over medium flame. Add the agar agar. Stir the pieces around until they melt (about 7 minutes).

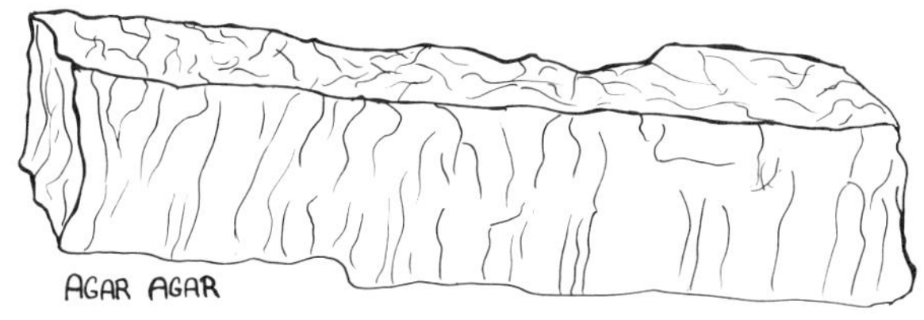

3. Wash the strawberries. Cut off the green tops. Slice each strawberry into about 4 pieces.
4. After the agar agar is melted, add the strawberries and cook on low flame for 5 minutes.
5. Pour the liquid into a bowl. Let it cool for a few minutes. Then put it in the refrigerator until it sets (about 1 hour).
6. Top with a pinch of fresh or dried mint. Serves 4. A delicious taste treat for spring and summer.

To make the jello like a custard, follow the above recipe until step 5. Then pour the cooked jello into a blender. Turn the blender to a low speed and blend the jello for 3 or 4 minutes. Then pour in a dessert dish and chill in the refrigerator.

Count on 20 minutes to prepare, plus 1 hour chilling time

B. INGREDIENTS

       1 package or 1 tablespoon unflavored
            gelatine
    1 ⅓ cups unsweetened apple juice
      ½ pint or about 15 strawberries
         pinch of dried or fresh mint

WHAT TO DO

1. Place ½ cup apple juice in the pot. Sprinkle gelatine over the apple juice. Heat over a low flame.
2. When gelatine dissolves, add remaining 1¼ cups apple juice.
3. Wash strawberries. Cut off the green tops. Slice each strawberry into about 4 pieces. Add to gelatine.
4. Continue to heat mixture until it starts to boil, but do not let it boil. Turn off the flame.
5. Pour into bowl. Allow to cool for a few minutes. Chill in the refrigerator until jello is firm. Top with crushed mint. Serves 4.

WHIPPED CREAM

There's something extra special about a dessert topped with your own homemade whipped cream. And all you need is heavy cream. It's great over sliced fresh fruit, especially strawberries, or any dessert in this section.

Count on 20 minutes with a hand beater or 8 minutes with an electric mixer, plus an hour chilling time

INGREDIENTS

    1 pint heavy cream
   ¼ teaspoon vanilla (optional)
   ¼ teaspoon cinnamon (optional)
    1 teaspoon honey (optional)

YOU'LL ALSO NEED

    1 mixing bowl (medium)
    1 egg beater or electric mixer
    1 set measuring spoons

WHAT TO DO

1. Chill the bowl and the egg beater in the refrigerator for about an hour before you are ready to make the whipped cream.
2. Pour the heavy cream into the bowl. Mix in the vanilla and cinnamon if you are going to use them.
3. Start to beat or whip the cream. If you do it with an egg beater, it will take about 15 or 20 minutes for the cream to get thick. Have patience and keep beating. It's worth

it. If you can, use an electric mixer. It should take about 5 minutes on a low speed to whip the cream.

4. If you like sweet whipped cream, add the honey when the cream begins to thicken. I don't use honey because the dessert itself is usually sweet enough.

5. When the cream is thick, put a spoonful on top of each dessert. Don't forget to lick the bowl. Enough for 4 desserts.

SNACKS AND EXTRAS

This section is purely for fun—healthy fun. It's for those times when you get a yen or a craving or a desire for something extra to munch on. Nothing tastes better than your own cookies and candy. Try making your own popcorn and taking it with you to the movies. Or crunch on it while playing at home.

Just remember not to eat too much of any snack so that you spoil your appetite for the next meal.

And now to the kitchen.

ROASTED SEEDS

A tasty, crunchy snack. Whenever you prepare pumpkin or squash, save the seeds and roast them. Also try this recipe with sunflower seeds.

Count on 20 minutes from start to finish

INGREDIENTS

½ pound pumpkin seeds or sunflower seeds
3 tablespoons tamari
2 tablespoons water
1 teaspoon corn oil

YOU'LL ALSO NEED

1 cookie sheet (11 inches by 16 inches)
1 bowl (medium)
1 measuring cup
1 set measuring spoons
1 pastry brush or piece of paper towel

WHAT TO DO

1. Preheat oven to 350° F.
2. Pour tamari into a bowl. Mix it with the water.
3. Mix seeds in tamari.
4. Oil a cookie sheet.
5. Spread seeds out on cookie sheet.
6. Bake in oven for 15 minutes.
7. Put seeds into a bowl. Nibble when hungry. Makes a medium bowlful, or fills a few small stomachs.

OATMEAL RAISIN COOKIES

Count on 45 minutes from start to finish

INGREDIENTS

1 ½ cups rolled oats
1 ½ cups whole wheat pastry flour
1 teaspoon salt
3 tablespoons corn oil
1 teaspoon cinnamon
¼ cup currants or raisins
3 tablespoons sunflower seeds or raw cashews
1 ½ cups unsweetened apple juice or 1 ½ cups
water plus 3 tablespoons honey
2 teaspoons oil

YOU'LL ALSO NEED

1 measuring cup
1 set measuring spoons
1 bowl (large)
2 cookie sheets (11 inches by 16 inches)
1 pastry brush or piece of paper towel
1 wooden spoon

WHAT TO DO

1. Preheat oven to 400° F.
2. Mix the oats and flour together in a bowl.
3. Add salt. Mix in oil. Smooth out any lumps by rubbing the mixture between your hands.
4. Add currants or raisins, sunflower seeds or cashews, and cinnamon. Mix all together.

5. Mix in apple juice and water, stirring with spoon while pouring it in. Make sure all the ingredients are mixed well.
6. Oil the cookie sheets.
7. Take a spoonful of batter and place it on the cookie sheet. The cookies should be about 2 inches round. Three spoonfuls of batter should fit on each row. You should come out with 4 rows on each cookie sheet.
8. Bake the cookies in a 400° F oven until they are crisp (about 30 minutes). You've made 2 dozen or 24 crunchy cookies.

TUESDAY NIGHT COCONUT COOKIES

Named for the Tuesday night my cooking class turned left-over pancake batter into coconut cookies.

Count on 45 minutes from start to finish

INGREDIENTS

⅔ cups corn flour
⅔ cups whole wheat pastry flour
⅔ cups rolled oats
1 teaspoon salt
1 cup water
1 cup unsweetened shredded coconut
½ cup raw cashews
¼ cup honey
a few raisins

YOU'LL ALSO NEED

1 mixing bowl (large)
1 measuring cup
1 set measuring spoons
1 pastry brush or piece of paper towel
2 cookie sheets (11 inches by 16 inches)
1 knife

WHAT TO DO

1. Preheat oven to 375° F.
2. Mix flours, oats, and salt in a mixing bowl.
3. Cut cashews into small pieces. Add to flour mixture.

4. Mix in coconut and honey.
5. Stir in water slowly.
6. Oil the cookie sheets.
7. Spoon the cookie mixture onto the cookie sheet. Make the cookies as large or small as you like.
8. Make raisin designs like faces, stars, or circles on the top of each cookie by sticking the raisins into the cookie batter.
9. Bake in oven for 30 minutes. Makes about 20 crunchy cookies.

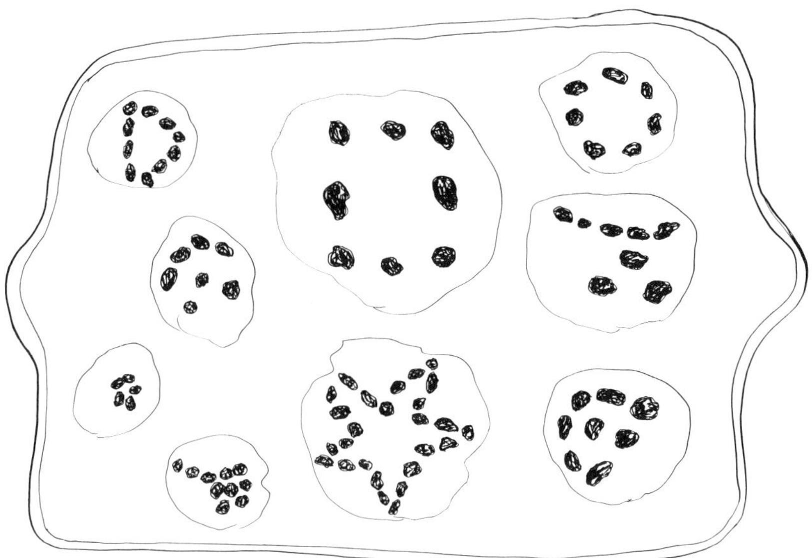

CREAM CHEESE CANDY

This is fast, easy, and needs no cooking.

Count on 10 minutes to fix, 15 minutes to harden

INGREDIENTS

  1 large package cream cheese (8 ounces)
  2 teaspoons milk (optional)
  1 tablespoon honey
10 walnuts without the shells (optional)
  1 teaspoon vanilla
  ½ cup unsweetened, shredded coconut

YOU'LL ALSO NEED

1 bowl (large)
1 set measuring spoons
1 measuring cup
1 spoon
1 knife and cutting board (for walnuts)

WHAT TO DO

1. Put cream cheese in the bowl. Add the milk. Mash the cream cheese with a spoon until milk is mixed in.
2. Add the vanilla and honey. If you are going to use walnuts, chop them into small pieces. Mix them in. Make sure all ingredients are well blended.
3. Pour coconut onto a flat plate. Form the cream cheese into balls. Roll them in the cocount.
4. Put the balls on a dish. Place dish in the refrigerator. Let candy harden for about 15 minutes.
5. It's all ready to eat. Makes about 12 pieces.

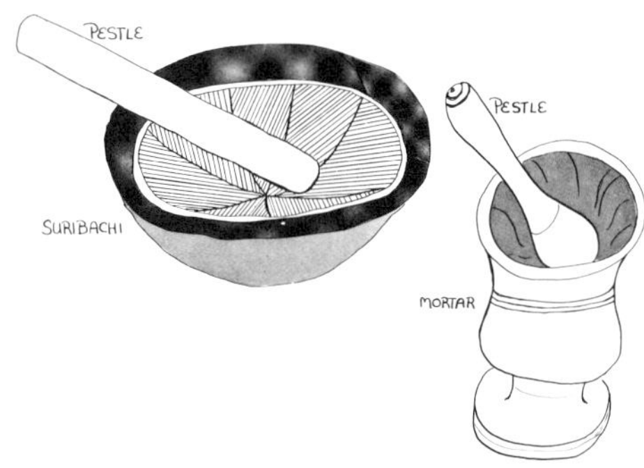

SESAME SALT

Sesame salt livens up the taste of almost any food—salads, rice, vegetables, soups, or cereals. It is also good for you because sesame seeds contain protein. It isn't even very salty because when you crush the sesame seeds, oil comes out of them and takes away the salty taste. It's also fun to make.

Count on 30 minutes from start to finish

INGREDIENTS

      1 teaspoon sea salt
      4 tablespoons sesame seeds (unhulled)

YOU'LL ALSO NEED

      1 suribachi (Japanese grating bowl that can be bought in a health food store or where Japanese food is sold) and a pestle
      or 1 blender
      or 1 mortar and pestle
      1 skillet (small)
      1 strainer (fine holes)
      1 wooden chopstick

WHAT TO DO

1. Measure out the sea salt. Put it in a skillet. Place a medium flame under it. Stir with a chopstick. Turn flame off after about 3 minutes. Place salt in suribachi or mortar or blender.

2. Measure out sesame seeds, Place them in a strainer with very small holes so that they don't fall through. Run water through the strainer and pick out any pieces that look like dirt. Wash the seeds this way a few times. Then put sesame seeds in the skillet. Place medium flame under it and stir with a chopstick so seeds won't burn. Heat them until they begin to turn brown and start to pop. They are ready when you can easily crush one between your fingers.

3. Place toasted sesame seeds into suribachi or mortar or blender. The idea is to grind the salt and sesame seeds together until they are crushed. Place blender on low or medium speed and grind until seeds are almost crushed (about 3 minutes). If you're using a suribachi or mortar, crush the seeds by pressing the pestle into the seeds and turning it around the bowl. You don't need to press very hard. Take your time and make sure you are patient. I like to do it by hand because it's old-fashioned and makes me feel like I'm doing it all myself.

After the sesame salt is ready, put it in an airtight jar with a cover. This keeps the salt fresh. It will stay fresh and crunchy for about a week. Keep it on the table so people can use as much as they like with whatever they're eating. This much sesame salt should last a family of four about a week.

POPCORN

Count on 15 minutes from start to finish

INGREDIENTS

½ cup dried corn kernels (popcorn)

1 or 2 tablespoons corn oil

½ teaspoon salt

2 tablespoons corn oil or 1 tablespoon butter to
   put on popcorn after it's cooked

YOU'LL ALSO NEED

1 pot with cover (8 ½ inches wide, 4 inches deep
   is a good size)

1 measuring cup

1 set measuring spoons

2 potholders

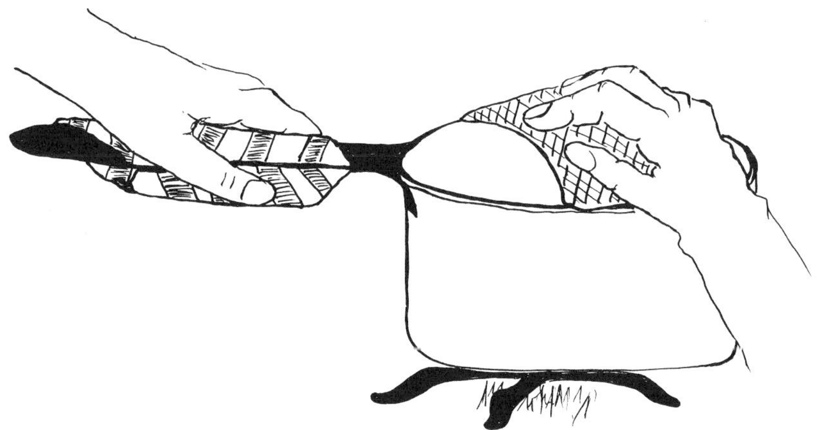

WHAT TO DO

1. Pour oil into the bottom of the pan. Use enough to cover the bottom. Heat it over a medium flame.
2. Pour in the popcorn kernels carefully. Cover.
3. When you hear popping noises, use a potholder to hold the pot handle and shake the pot. Use the other potholder to hold the cover of the pot while you're shaking it. Do this several times.
4. When the popping noise stops, the popcorn is ready (about 10 minutes).
5. Turn off the flame. Let the pot sit about 3 minutes to make sure it has stopped popping.
6. Mix in the salt and butter or oil. (You'd be surprised how good oil tastes over popcorn.)
7. Serve. Makes a large bowlful which usually doesn't last long.

QUICKLIES: IDEAS THAT DON'T NEED COOKING

1. If you're looking for a lunch idea, try *cottage cheese* and *blueberries.*

2. A do-it-yourself *ice cream sundae* idea. Top your favorite ice cream with honey or maple syrup and chopped walnuts. Then pile on your homemade whipped cream.

3. Put this together yourself in just 5 minutes. Mix some raw cashews and peanuts with sunflower seeds, raisins, or dried apricots. Hikers call this mixture *Gorp.* Use your imagination and mix any combination of seeds, nuts, and dried fruits.

4. This is called a *Gooey Apple.* Pour some honey into a bowl. Stick a pointy chopstick into the top of the apple. Dip the apple into the honey. Place the apple on a piece of wax paper or aluminum foil. Let it harden in the refrigerator for ½ hour. Bite in.

5. Cut a *date* in half. Take out the pit. Spread both halves of the date with *cream cheese.* Zip it into your mouth.

6. Try the recipe for *cream cheese candy.* It's a mouth-melter.

DRINKS

A good beverage is really just a liquid form of food. It should be good for you as well as quench your thirst.

Different beverages make you feel different ways. Sweet ones give you energy. But remember there are ways to make your drinks sweet without using sugar. Drinks like herb teas are soothing and can help you to feel calm and quiet.

There are times when beverages feel like a best friend, especially after a sweaty game of baseball or jump rope. When you're thirsty, remember not to drink too fast or too much. Also, make sure whatever you're drinking is not too hot or too cold. The test is whether it goes down smooth and easy.

Drinks also vary with the time of year. You've probably noticed that in the summer you feel like drinking liquids that are cool and refreshing. But in the winter you want hot drinks that warm you up.

In this section you'll find a few of each.

Bottoms up.

CREAMIEST MILK SHAKE

Takes 10 minutes from start to finish

INGREDIENTS

- 4 cups milk
- 1 apple
- 2 tablespoons honey
- 1 teaspoon vanilla
- 1 teaspoon cinnamon

YOU'LL ALSO NEED

- 1 cutting board
- 1 measuring cup
- 1 blender
- 1 set measuring spoons
- 1 corer
- 1 knife

WHAT TO DO

1. Wash the apple. Peel and core it. Slice and dice it.
2. Place milk, diced apple, and other ingredients into the blender.
3. Blend on a low speed for 3 minutes.
4. Pour into glasses. Serves 4. Drink immediately.

HERB TEAS

Many herbs and plants are used to make teas. Some of them are camomile flowers, sassafras bark, strawberry, mint, and raspberry leaves, and the leaves and twigs of the bancha bush. These plants and herbs don't contain any caffein, which is the ingredient in coffee that makes you jumpy. They are usually sold loose rather than in tea bags. Herb teas are good for you and they taste good too.

It is handy to use a tea strainer when you make tea. A strainer prevents the tea leaves from falling into the tea. There are two different types of strainers. One is a metal ball with small holes in it. The ball is divided into two halves. You place the tea inside one half and then fit both halves together. You make the tea by putting the ball into a pot of water.

The other kind of strainer is a tiny version of the large one you use to drain foods like spaghetti. To use this kind of

118

strainer place the tea inside it. Then place the strainer in a tea cup. Pour freshly boiled water through the strainer until the cup is almost full. Be sure to use a potholder when pouring the hot water. This kind of strainer can only be used for teas that need to be steeped or soaked but don't need to be cooked.

There are also two different ways to prepare teas. When you use teas made of flowers or thin leaves you need only soak them in boiling water. Do this with camomile flowers, mint, strawberry, and raspberry leaves. Use 1 teaspoon of tea for each cup of water. Place the tea in a strainer and soak it in freshly boiled water for about 3 minutes. When you make teas out of treebark or leaves and twigs like sassafras or bancha, place the tea in the teaball and let it cook in gently boiling water for about 10 minutes. Then you are ready to serve it. Use ½ teaspoon tea for each cup of water.

If you use an herb teabag prepare it the same way you would an ordinary teabag.

ICED HERB TEA

A great summer drink.

Count on 15 minutes to make the tea, plus 1 hour to chill it

INGREDIENTS

    1 teaspoon tea for each cup water
    1 teaspoon honey for each cup water (optional)
    1 cup water for each cup of tea
    ice cubes

YOU'LL ALSO NEED

    1 teapot or regular pot
    1 set measuring spoons
    1 tea strainer
    1 pitcher or glasses

WHAT TO DO

1. Decide how many cups of iced tea you want to make. Extra tea will stay fresh for a few days if you keep it in the refrigerator.
2. If you want to make 4 cups of tea, boil 4 cups of water. After the water boils, either steep or boil the tea, depending on the kind you are using (see Herb Tea recipe p. 118). The darker the color turns, the stronger the tea will be. Decide how strong you like it.
3. Add the honey if you like sweet tea. Mix it well. Pour it into a pitcher. Put it in the refrigerator for about an hour to chill.

4. Add 2 or 3 ice cubes to each glass or put the ice cubes in a pitcher. Pour in the tea. Serve. It's refreshing.

ORANGE FROTH

Count on 7 or 8 minutes from start to finish

INGREDIENTS

    4 oranges
  1 ⅓ cups unsweetened apple juice

YOU'LL ALSO NEED

    1 blender
    1 measuring cup

WHAT TO DO

1. Peel oranges. Separate the sections. Remove pits. Place in blender.
2. Place apple juice in blender.
3. Blend at low speed for 2 minutes. Drink immediately.
4. Makes 4 glasses of frothy orange drink.

LEMONADE

It's easy to make your own.

Count on 5 minutes to make, plus 1 hour to cool

INGREDIENTS

    4 cups water
    3 or 4 teaspoons honey
    1 lemon
       ice cubes

YOU'LL ALSO NEED

    1 pot (medium)
    1 set measuring spoons
    1 pitcher or 6 glasses

WHAT TO DO

1. Boil the water. Turn off the flame.
2. Cut the lemon into 4 parts. Remove pits. Squeeze each part into the hot water. Drop the rind into the water, too.
3. Measure out the honey. Mix it into the water.
4. Pour the mixture into a pitcher. Put it in the refrigerator. Let it cool for about an hour. Take out the rinds.
5. Put 2 or 3 ice cubes into each glass. Pour in the lemonade and serve. Enough for 6.

122

THOUGHTFUL TEA

Mu tea is a very special tea that contains sixteen different herbs. It is very hearty tasting, so a little bit goes a long way. Mu tea can be bought in a health food store and makes a good winter drink that warms you through and through.

Takes a little over 10 minutes from start to finish

INGREDIENTS

    1 Mu tea bag
    4 cups water
    1 cup apple juice
      pinch of cinnamon or 1 cinnamon stick

YOU'LL ALSO NEED

    1 teapot or pot with cover (medium)
    1 measuring cup
    1 spoon

WHAT TO DO

1. Bring water to a boil.
2. Drop in Mu tea bag. Let it simmer for 5 minutes.
3. Lift out Mu tea bag carefully with a spoon. Mix in the apple juice. Heat for about 3 minutes on medium flame.
4. Mix in a pinch of cinnamon or serve in a large pitcher with a cinnamon stick floating in it. Enough for 4, maybe more.

AFTERWORD

Now that you know the basics, it's all up to you. Experiment. If you get an idea, try it. Listen to what people call your instinct. That's the secret voice inside you that makes suggestions about how you should do things. Enjoy every moment when you cook.

GLOSSARY

(The Place That Tells You Word Meanings)

Arrowroot A powder used in place of cornstarch. It comes from the arrowroot plant. It is used to thicken soups, sauces, and desserts.

Baking A way of cooking in which food is put into an oven and is cooked by the heat that is all around it.

Batter A mixture of flour and a liquid like milk or water, which is used to make pancakes and cakes.

Beverage A drink.

Boil To heat a liquid or solid food to a point where bubbles form.

Broil A way to cook food in which the food is placed directly underneath the heat.

Casserole Food cooked in a covered baking dish and usually served in the same dish it is cooked in.

Chemical A substance used to change another substance. For example, when chemicals are added to food they may change the color or flavor of the food or make it last longer.

Cereal A food made from a grain. It is usually soft because it is cooked in liquid.

Chop To cut into pieces with a knife.

Clove One bud or section of a whole, like garlic. Another kind of clove is an East Indian spice.

Colander A bowl with holes in the sides and bottom. It is used to drain food.

Core The center of something. When you core a fruit like an apple, you take out the center part that contains the seeds.

Dice To cut into small squares. For instructions, see the recipe for Vegetable Pancakes p. 58.

Dilute To mix a food with a liquid so that the food becomes weaker or thinner. For instance, mixing tamari with water makes it less salty.

Dissolve To mix something solid like a powder into a liquid so that the solid part disappears. For example, when you mix arrowroot into water, you get a milky-colored liquid.

Fry To cook food by placing it on top of the heat. When you fry food you usually use some kind of fat or oil.

Gadget A small mechanical object.

Garlic press A small metal object with holes that is used to squeeze garlic.

Herbs Plants that are used for seasoning, like thyme, rosemary, sage, and parsley, as well as many others.

Ingredients The various foods that go into preparing a recipe.

Lengthwise The long way. In these recipes it means to cut a food the long way from the top to the bottom.

Method A way to do something.

Mince To cut into small pieces.

Mixture A combination of different ingredients.

Mortar A bowl in which substances are mashed or ground. It is usually used with a pestle, which is the stick that grinds the substance.

Nutrients Substances found in food, like vitamins, proteins, carbohydrates, fats, and minerals that help to keep your body healthy.

Nutritious Something that adds to good health.

Optional Means you can decide whether you want to put it in or leave it out.

Organic food Food that is grown without using chemicals or poisonous sprays.

Pan fry To cook food by frying it in a pan.

Pinch As much as you can hold between your thumb and the tip of another finger.

Poach To cook food in liquid that is boiling gently or simmering.

Preheat To heat the oven to the temperature you want to cook a food before you actually start. The "F." after the temperature in a recipe means Fahrenheit, which is the standard measure of heat used in all ovens. The ° means degrees.

Preservative A substance added to food to make it last longer. Some that are used in foods today may be harmful to eat.

Recipe Directions which tell you how to cook a particular dish or food.

Refined food Food that is changed from its original state until it is lighter in color or weight, such as white sugar.

Ripe All grown up and ready to eat.

Sauté To cook a food quickly in a little oil.

Simmer To cook food at a very gentle boil.

Skillet A frying pan.

Spatula A square looking flat piece with a handle. Used to pick up foods and turn them over.

Spice A vegetable or plant used in cooking which adds a hot or burning taste to food. For example, pepper or ginger.

Sprig A piece of a plant that contains the stem and flower part. For instance, a sprig of parsley.

Sprinkling A few drops of a certain food.

Stalk The stem or long part of a plant or vegetable like celery.

Steam A way of cooking in which the food is placed above a small amount of boiling water, not in it. The food gets cooked by the steam or heat that rises from the water.

Suribachi A Japanese bowl with special sides that is used for grating or mashing.

Tamari A pure kind of soy sauce that is made from soybeans, wheat, sea salt, and water.

Vitamins Substances found in food which you need in order to be healthy, such as vitamins A, B, C, D, and many others.

Wedge A block in the shape of a triangle. For example, a wedge of cheese.

Whole grain The whole seed of certain plants like wheat, barley, rye, corn, rice, millet, or oats.

Wok A Chinese pan with a round bottom used for cooking food on a high flame in a short time.